# RÖLVAAG

O. E. Rölvaag a few months before his death in 1931.

# RÖLVAAG

## *his life and art*

## *PAUL REIGSTAD*

*university of nebraska press • lincoln*

Publishers on the Plains

**UNP**

Copyright © 1972 by the University of Nebraska Press
All rights reserved
International Standard Book Number 0–8032–0803–0
Library of Congress Catalog Card Number 70–175804


Most recent printing shown by first digit below:
1    2    3    4    5    6    7    8    9    10


Manufactured in the United States of America

*For Marjorie, Emily, and Katharine*

# CONTENTS

*A picture section follows page 64.*

# PREFACE

$O$nly one full-length study of O. E. Rölvaag has been published, a book written more than thirty years ago by two of his colleagues at St. Olaf College, Theodore Jorgenson and Nora Solum. Their book is an excellent biography, full of the minutiae of an interesting life. But it is not an entirely satisfactory literary study, being disproportionately concerned with Rölvaag as political and cultural spokesman for Norwegians in America.

A survey of Rölvaag criticism since the publication of that biography reveals that most of it has been produced by social scientists, who have focused attention upon his novels as lively historical assessments of the cost of immigration and the westward movement. To these critics Rölvaag's voice is prophetic, his achievement dazzling. In the words of Theodore Blegen, "With more insight and deeper power than almost any writer, he recorded and interpreted the American transition of the immigrants who made their way in the western world."

Unquestionably, there is truth in the assertion. *Giants in the Earth* is generally regarded as one of the two or three best fictional delineations of pioneer life on the prairies, and Rölvaag is recognized as an innovator capable of consummate artistry. But in practice he is often dismissed after being accorded such high praise. Part of the problem may be that his admirers claim too great an achievement for him.

My concern is with Rölvaag the novelist, rather than with Rölvaag the historian or prophet of acculturation, and I hope that my study will serve as an introduction to his novels. I have used

*ix*

such biographical data as seemed necessary to understand his artistic development and to provide a context for his literary activity. Although I do not conclude with some enthusiasts that Rölvaag's contribution to American literature is monumentally important, it seems certain that *Giants in the Earth* has attained the stature of a minor classic. Furthermore, several of the other novels, though less successful as works of art, are worthy of careful attention.

A writer as original as Rölvaag deserves continuing appraisal. My study seeks to fulfill this need.

PAUL REIGSTAD

*Pacific Lutheran University*

# ACKNOWLEDGMENTS

*I* want to thank my friend and teacher, Professor George Arms of the University of New Mexico, for sharing my interest in Rölvaag and encouraging me to carry out this project. I also want to thank several organizations which supported my work through research grants: The American-Scandinavian Foundation, The American Philosophical Society, and The American Lutheran Church.

Without the cooperation of the Rölvaag family—especially the author's widow, now deceased—I should not have had access to the material in the family archives which is largely responsible for whatever value this study has. Both Karl Rolvaag and his sister, Ella Valborg Tweet, supplied me with helpful information and in other ways facilitated the completion of this study. For their generous permission to quote from unpublished letters and manuscripts I am deeply grateful.

I am also indebted to Mrs. Rölvaag for her assistance with difficult translations, as I am to Mrs. O. H. Nelson; to Mrs. C. F. Nickerson for allowing me to read her unpublished translation of *On Forgotten Paths;* and to Katherine Floyd and my daughter Emily for cheerfully typing the manuscript.

I am most grateful of all to my wife, Marjorie, whose confidence brought this book into being.

*RÖLVAAG*

# *1*

# ROOTS IN THE HOMELAND

Dönna Island, the childhood home of Ole Edvart Rölvaag, lies along the Helgeland coast of northern Norway just below the Arctic Circle. Its mountainous southern tip is spotted with modest stands of pine and dwarf birch, but the northern portion, where Rölvaag lived, is largely flat and barren, covered with heather, moss, and peat bogs. Scarcely a tree is to be seen except those which have been planted, and the few that have managed to sink roots among the rocks are stunted and twisted. The hamlet of Rölvaag[1] lies along the northwestern shore of Dönna, not directly on open water but on a narrow finger of the sea which pushes inward through a volcanic fissure. Behind the Rölvaag cottage rises a low bony ridge which the boy liked to climb and from which he could look westward to the sea, wondering about the magic land beyond.

Ole Edvart, born April 22, 1876, was one of the seven children of Peder Jakobsen Rölvaag and Ellerine Pedersdatter Vaag. Though the family and most of its forebears were uneducated cottagers and fishermen, there were clear evidences among them of wit and intellectual vigor and sometimes a proclivity for storytelling. Ole and his older brother, particularly, inherited the family love of reading and were among the most enthusiastic patrons of the small local library, in which, according to Rölvaag's boyhood friend John Heitmann, "a majority of the well-known names of world

---

1. In keeping with an old Norwegian custom, Rölvaag took his name from his birthplace.

literature were represented, not only in fiction and poetry, but
also in history, biography, art, travel, philosophy, and the sciences."[2]
Rölvaag's personality reflected both his father's logical and questioning mind and his mother's imaginative response to the elemental beauty and mystery of Nordland life.

The home in which he was born, an ancient timber cottage
with a sod roof, had been occupied by his ancestors for six generations. With roots so deep, the family felt keenly a primitive sense
of belonging—an awareness so powerful in Rölvaag that the main
concern in his writing was to show the depths of those roots which
immigrants wrenched from native soil and the inability of some
of them ever to belong spiritually to the New World. In his unfinished and unpublished autobiography[3] Rölvaag tells us that the
west shore of the cove where he lived has been inhabited since
prehistoric days. He knew well the path "to the boatlanding [ . . . ][4]
worn down into the very rocks by the iron-clad heels of the heavy
seaboots that have tramped there, up and down, down and up,
from time immemorial." Part of the Dönnes church which the
Rölvaag family attended was built in the twelfth century, and
in its churchyard are buried the ancestors of the present inhabitants

2. John Heitmann, "Ole Edvart Rölvaag," *Norwegian-American Studies and
Records* 12 (1941): 153.

3. O. E. Rölvaag, "The Romance of a Life." Unless otherwise indicated, all
Rölvaag quotations in chapter 1 are from this autobiographical fragment, one
of Rölvaag's few literary works in English. About two-thirds of the lines are
printed here for the first time; the remainder also appear in Theodore Jorgenson
and Nora Solum, *Ole Edvart Rölvaag: A Biography* (New York: Harper and
Brothers Publishers, 1939). The autobiography and other primary materials on
which this study is based are in the Rölvaag Collection, Archives of the Norwegian-American Historical Association, St. Olaf College, Northfield, Minnesota.
Unless otherwise noted, all of the writings cited are in the Rölvaag Collection,
which includes letters, class notes, clippings, lectures, and holograph manuscripts of all the novels. I have corrected errors in spelling and grammar, and
occasionally in punctuation, in Rölvaag's English writings, especially the earliest
letters.

4. Because Rölvaag frequently uses ellipses as a stylistic device, I have indicated
omissions—from his work only—by suspension points in brackets.

of the hamlet. It is not strange that the Dönna fishermen feel strong ties with such a venerable institution.

Rölvaag was twenty years old when he emigrated to America; to those twenty years of life in Nordland can be traced most of the influences which unalterably shaped his mind and art. The strongest of them was the spectacular natural beauty of his surroundings, particularly mountains, sea, and arctic summer and winter. As a boy he was steeped in the belief that the world about him was full of living spirits. The mountains, particularly, had a being of their own, and, as he records in his autobiography, on "dark and rainy days in the late fall, [they] put on wet clothes and wrapped banks of fog about their heads; then they looked foreboding in their mighty isolation. They must know terrible secrets, I thought." He imagined that the spirit of the mountains entered into his daily life—watched over him and could be fearsome or glad. "By and by there sprang up a great intimacy between me and the mountains. After I got so big that I could handle a boat alone we became good friends."

The farmers and fishermen interpreted the world about them much as their ancestors had in pagan and early Christian days. Legends and ballads reflected the traditions and mood of the old Germanic poetry, inheriting from the sagas the techniques of vivid characterization and subtle psychological delineation. From the fairy tales came the supernatural creatures—trolls, gnomes, giants—and the stock characters and situations of Norwegian folk literature. Particularly the peasants loved to hear and tell tales of the *askeladd,* or ash-lad, a kind of male Cinderella who rises to distinction from an unpromising youth—like his distant relative, Beowulf.

It is no accident that in Norwegian literature, the climbing of a mountain frequently symbolizes human aspiration. Forbidding peaks and desolate snowfields inevitably suggest the struggle for attainment. In Ibsen's plays attainment often seems impossible, and man is doomed to failure, though he must aspire. However, there is also a native Norwegian optimism, expressed most clearly in the folk tales. Björnstjerne Björnson in the novel *Arne* tells the old story of how the mountain was clad. After being defeated in its attempt to clothe the craggy heights, the juniper tackles the job in another spirit: "Very well, if you won't have me, *I'll* have *you!*"[5] This same determination is expressed in the fairy tale "The Glass Mountain," which tells of a princess, seated on the top of a glass mountain, waiting to be given in marriage to the suitor who can scale the heights. On the third try a servant boy—the familiar ash-lad—reaches her and wins the prize. The boy Rölvaag knew these tales well and dreamed of being himself the *askeladd* who would some day scale the heights or discover the secrets beyond the sea.

The mountains visible from Dönna were invariably incarnations of powerful forces: Hestmanden (The Horseman) to the north, rising precipitously from the Norwegian Sea and shining in the golden light of early morning, was a powerful mounted horseman in motion; and Syv Söstre (Seven Sisters) to the east, though troll maidens turned to stone, still exercised their evil powers. Only Dönnmannen (The Man of Dönna), on the southern tip of the island, was lifeless—a rock ridge shaped like a man lying dead.

Hestmanden, particularly, fascinated the peasants and fishermen. Jonas Lie, whom Rölvaag loved above all other novelists, writes of the sheer poetry of The Horseman on a stormy night, "with its height of 1700 feet, riding southwards out in the surf, while his cloak fluttered from his shoulder toward the north, and, besides the giant himself in his might . . . the horse's head, his ear, his neck, his snaffle, and his majestic chest."[6]

In his autobiography Rölvaag recalls the legend of Hestmanden as he first heard it and as it was prevalent among the Nordlændings:

5. Björnstjerne Björnson, "How the Mountain Was Clad," in *Norway's Best Stories,* ed. Hanna Astrup Larsen (New York: W. W. Norton and Company, 1927), pp. 3–7.

6. Jonas Lie, *The Visionary; or Pictures from Nordland,* trans. Jessie Muir (London: Hodder Brothers, 1894), p. 37.

*4*

## Roots in the Homeland

Once upon a time a fierce giant had his home in Hestman-den; he was madly in love with a troll maiden called Lækka-möya, the Maiden of Lækka, who abode in a mountain some eighty miles to the south. Though she had only "No" to all his wooing, still he would persist to see her. One night he kept on entreating too long, and in a fit of peevishness he reached out with his hand to a mountain some distance to the east; breaking off a huge rock, he whirled it at the maiden. So terrible was the force of the heave that the rock went right through a mountain standing in the way, cutting a hole through it some seventy-five feet square. That mountain is called Torghatten—the hat of Torg—and with hole and all is to this day one of the wonders of the world. But that it never pays to get mad Hest-manden was to learn on this occasion, for the stone-throwing had delayed him in getting back home, and before he could get himself underground, the rays of the morning sun struck him and turned him into a huge mass of solid rock. There he has been standing to this day. Whenever a storm rages from the north, he is fierce to look at, for then, usually, fog gathers round his head; you see it floating in the air like a veil.

Even closer than his friendship with the mountains was the kin-ship Rölvaag felt with the sea; it was the central fact of the boy's existence. Many years after leaving Norway, he wrote to his fiancée of the importance of the sea in his life:

I can almost say that during my entire childhood I lived in battle with the North Sea [Norwegian Sea]. That battle has left an ineffaceable mark upon me; the passion in my soul is as strong as the storms there in the north. [. . .] The Rölvaag boys are afraid of neither wind nor weather, people say, and that is almost true because there was no fear in any of us. Scarcely any wave was too high for us or any storm too strong. We always came out on top. Oh yes, many times we were in danger of death; that things turned out so well was surely due to God's love and Mother's prayers. [. . .] I can still remember well how I liked to take my hat off when the wind was strong and let the wind ruffle my hair and the rain lash my face.[7]

---

7. Rölvaag to Jennie Berdahl, September 22, 1904 (trans. from Norwegian). Here and elsewhere all translations are the author's unless otherwise indicated.

His childhood was filled with stories of supernatural creatures of the deep: Leviathan, Behemoth, the mermaid—and the sea serpent which his own father, who was not a liar, had seen. Most fearful of all were the tales about the *draug,* an apparition of a headless man, often in a half-boat, whose dread appearance portends disaster, usually either shipwreck or drowning. The sea was immediate, the source of the fisherman's sustenance. "Upon the sea I lived, most of the time; about it my dream-life was woven; for the sea was at one and the same time the most vital reality and the unfathomable mystery." The most terrifying aspect of the sea was its fury. Lying in bed listening to the rumble of the sea raging beyond the skerries, the boy thought of the Last Judgment. Sometimes in winter stormy spells lasted for weeks, destroying property and life. But calm days always returned, and he was happiest when he could climb into the boat and row out of the bay.

Rölvaag learned early the tragedy common to men who live on the sea; though drownings were not frequent among the seasoned fishermen, those that occurred left vivid memories. He remembered standing on Lookout Hill one day when he was six years old and seeing three men drown, one of them his closest neighbor:

> There was no one near enough to give rescue. The incident is branded in my memory; I need only close my eyes to live again the sad scene—the murky day in late fall, the stirred-up sea, and the three men trying desperately to hang on to a capsized boat in a heavy sea, only to be washed away one after the other. I can yet hear the frantic cries of the women.

On another occasion he was forced to stand by helplessly as his little brother struggled in the sea:

> Out in the bay our boat was adrift. [. . .] Andreas, hardly more than five, was hanging on to the gunwale with one hand, his body floating in the water; a northerly wind was standing out the bay, the waves rocking the boat dangerously. Suddenly I saw my oldest brother fling himself from the rocks into the rough waters, calling to Andreas to hold on for dear life. After a long pull he reached the boat and, putting his right hand

under the belly of the boy, he tipped him into the boat, then crawled in himself. By now the whole neighborhood had gathered on the brow of the ledge. Not a word was spoken. I remember how deathly pale Mother's face was and that she had to go to bed afterward.

That drownings were not more frequent among the children seemed strange to Rölvaag, for they played fearlessly in the cove and along its edge. He tells of a time when he fell asleep upon the rocks on a warm summer day "with a lazy lolling sea whispering dreamy tales to me. No one had missed me. There I lay till the incoming tide had set in, and I did not wake up before the sea had reached me and I was on the point of floating off."

To the boy the sea meant, above all, promise; and though he feared its savagery, he loved its variety and riches. He often watched the great whales blow their columns of vapor high into the air: "How they fascinated me: My first all-consuming ambition was to kill a whale. [ . . . ] I never mentioned this dream, not even to Mother, because I didn't want any of the grown-ups to get ahead of me." The sea was omnipotent and limitless, embracing the earth. Man's puny power against its might was like a breath in the hurricane that destroys whole cities. And it offered fabulous riches:

> Wasn't there in the cove of Rölvaag taken 7000 barrels of herring in one catch? Yet at times it might be so niggardly that we had to go hungry for weeks. When I listened to my big brother read Jules Verne my wonder and my awe for the sea grew, but also my love for it.

It was impossible for a boy so in love with the sea not to share its restlessness, not to yearn after its mystery; for as Rölvaag writes, whatever is taken within its mighty grasp, including a boy's spirit, "it presses ever onward, always and ever onward, round the wide girdle of the earth. [ . . . ] Out of itself, into itself—touching the heavens, sweeping the abysses, restlessly, endlessly into itself."[8]

---

8. O. E. Rölvaag, *The Boat of Longing*, trans. Nora Solum (New York: Harper and Brothers Publishers, 1933), p. 276.

Like Nils in Rölvaag's novel *The Boat of Longing,* he secretly dedicated himself to the highest of human endeavors, the creative life. As a college student in America many years later, Rölvaag recalled his youthful dedication to art:

> Loneliness had a tremendous power over me. I liked to be alone with my strong longings and dream of notable achievements; for I was certain that when I grew up I should accomplish great things. Once—I remember still as if it were yesterday —Mother asked me what I would be or wanted to be. Without a moment's reflection I answered, "Either a poet or a professor." You can imagine how she laughed, for how could a poor fisherlad become anything like that? But I was quite determined that it should be one or the other. Yes, yes, so many wonderful things happen in this world. Perhaps I may still have the opportunity to laugh at Mother because she once thought her own boy talked rank nonsense. She would surely be glad if that happened.[9]

In Norwegian folklore and balladry, discovering the beautiful Castle of Soria Moria symbolizes triumph. When a boy, Rölvaag found his own dream castle in the wondrous cloud formations that hung over the mountains in the shimmering Nordland summer evenings. His intense response to the mysterious beauty of life sought release in poetry, and he dreamed of writing songs. But his attempts could not still the restless yearning: "the lines would not come; after a while the song in my heart was as dead as the lines were. I could not understand how it could be because I had heard them so distinctly." He was certain he would die young, before singing the songs he was capable of creating.

Rölvaag lived in the land of the midnight sun, where for three months of the year there is no darkness at all, even at midnight. Then a strange beauty lies over the countryside bathed perpetually in light. But when the brief summer is spent, gloom gathers over a land increasingly gray and mist-shrouded. Storms often rage for

---

9. Rölvaag to Jennie Berdahl, September 22, 1904 (trans. from Norwegian).

days on end, lashing the sea into a fury which fills men's hearts with dread and turns their thoughts to the dark powers, which, since the time of the myths, have had their abode in the Far North. This frigid waste is the home of the ancient gods of evil, driven to the uttermost limits of earth by victorious Saint Olaf and there turned to stone. Late autumn, Rölvaag writes, is the time that people in the North mind most:

> It is as though some dark foreboding passes through nature and people alike, announcing that the sun is about to undertake a long journey from which it can never return. The fog is murkier, the rain more petulant and sour, and the storm wind more mournfully weird against the mountain walls. Even the grey cliffs get a more dismal look from staring into the desolation.[10]

In his autobiography Rölvaag remarks that darkness seems to give rise to more darkness. During the winter particularly, the people of the countryside talked of ghosts, superstitions, and ominous warnings. It was dangerous to stray far from home at any time, but especially at night. Among the spirits abroad were those of illegitimate infants, murdered before baptism by their fearful mothers. One of these might fling itself at the throat of a passer-by and strangle him unless he knew the proper charm:

> As late as the first half of the nineteenth century there existed among the common people a baptismal formula [. . .] which one must use in order to rid himself of the spirit.
> "Ann or John, no matter whom or how,
> I baptize thee here and now!"
> While making the sign of the cross the person was to repeat these words, and straightway the spirit would depart, never appearing again.

Ghosts were plentiful. About two miles from the Rölvaag home is an isolated lake visited only by an occasional herder. "Long before my time," Rölvaag writes, "a man by the name of Ingebret

---

10. Rölvaag, *The Boat of Longing*, p. 42.

had committed suicide by jumping into the lake. His body had never been found. But on dark nights strange cries and wailings could be heard coming out of the lake. That was the spirit of 'Old Ingebret' calling for help."

During the long Nordland winter, always gloomiest when little or no snow had fallen, gray mountains and skies pressed in upon the primitive dwellings. The restless inhabitants gathered around their stoves—the women knitting and the men mending nets—to tell stories, sober and grim usually, and nearly always tinged with the supernatural. In his autobiography, Rölvaag remembers a time—he was about twelve years old—when the herring fishing had been bad along their part of the coast. Nets set out at night caught only a sprinkling of fish, not more than enough to be used as bait for deep-sea fishing. Since there was little else that fisherman could do at that time of the year, several of them stayed in the Rölvaag home, waiting for their luck to turn. In the group were two men who appealed especially to the imaginative child, one of them his mother's cousin:

> He was a man who had once known comparative affluence but now was reduced to poverty because three winters ago he had lost a brand new Lofoten boat, and with it, his whole outfit of nets and tackle. Among the men staying with us was also Anders Dass, an old gray beard whom I worshipped because of his inexhaustable stock of good stories. *Arabian Nights* he knew better than the teacher knew his Catechism, and how he could tell! Almost every story he impersonated and dramatized. If the tale ended with a wedding, he himself had been the fiddler at the feast; invariably it was he that slew the dragon and carried off the princess. Many a fine öre piece [small Norwegian copper coin] did I pay him in order to get him to tell.
>
> One evening while the men were busy with their work and the women with theirs, Father talked around until he got our kinsman to tell his story of how he had lost his boat. Several of the others put in a word too and at last the man yielded. This is how the tragedy happened:
>
> It was a stormy night during Christmas, the wind whisking torn storm-clouds past a full moon as though they were hand-

fuls of eiderdown racing with the wind. The man was making himself ready to sail to the Lofoten Islands but had not yet taken his new boat out of the naust [boathouse]. He had already retired because he wasn't feeling well that night. The fierceness of the storm would not let him sleep; down the chimney the wind howled and oo-ed, around the corners it whined; into every crack and crevice it whistled making a draft in every room; from down by the shore came the fearful roar of the sea. Finally the man got up and dressed. With such a storm, should the tide rise much above normal, the boathouse would be in serious danger. Lighting his lantern he went down to the landing to see just how bad things were. As he approached he felt a shiver run through him; from the cracks between the boards in the boathouse he saw gleams of light. Who could be there now . . . on such a night . . . thieves helping themselves from his outfit? He swore terribly and neared stealthily. Finding a knot hole in the wall he put his eye to it; the sight he beheld made his blood curdle—a crew was working with the boat, and all of them headless men. Being more fearful for the safety of his new boat than for his own life he rushed to the door, unlocked it, and ran to the boathouse. There was much jeering and sneering and hullabaloo as that beastly crew was trying to lift the boat up on the runners preparatory to shoving it out through the door at the lower end of the boathouse. And above the wailings of the storm and the roar of the sea rose an unearthly call: "Hoi-oi, now lift ye all!" Beside himself with anger and fear the man shouted out: "To hell with you all and lift the devil! Leave my boat alone!" He had drawn the knife from his sheath and rushed at them and suddenly the air roared as if all the thunder had been unloosed in one great smash; the storm swept down upon the boathouse cracking it with its awful whip, rocking it to and fro as though it had been standing in a swing. Then all was still—so deadly still that you could have held a burning match in the air. With knees wobbling the man went to see about his boat—and there it was standing just as before. Cutting one cross into the stern and one into the prow and saying, "Father, Son, and Holy Ghost" for each one he climbed into the boat and slept in the stern that night. The next morning he could hardly drag himself home because he was burning with fever. This illness lasted for several weeks. It came sailing time; out in the ship's lane the whole fishing fleet came and shot by. For him there was nothing else to do than to place his most trusted man in charge and let the crew sail on with the boat, hoping that he might be so well later on that he could take the steamer to join them. Well, that never happened. Neither the boat nor the crew was ever heard of again!

Often with such tales as this fomenting in his mind the boy crawled into bed, the roar of the sea filling his ears and visions of ghostly visitants chilling his spirit.

Another of the forces contributing to Rölvaag's intellectual development was the Lutheran state church, which supervised all schools, including the universities. Reading was primarily of a devotional nature, and in the elementary grades the core of study was the catechism. As a result, theological dogmatism shaped the thinking of the people. Rölvaag in later life looked back with amusement upon some of the topics discussed in his home. His father especially became, as Jorgenson and Solum note, a "logician, stubborn and self-willed, fixed in his opinion and autocratic in his judgments,"[11] and in any theological argument he could hold his own.

Rölvaag met religious fanaticism in his everyday life, for among the farmers and fishermen, religion was aggressively pietistic. After his conversion in 1796, the Norwegian lay preacher and revivalist Hans Nielsen Hauge led a reaction against the absolutism of the established church and insisted upon the care of the individual soul. The roots of this reaction go back ultimately to the pietistic movement of seventeenth-century Germany, which called for reform in clergy and court to be brought about by a living faith manifested in upright conduct. Pietism, a term originally used in contempt, at its best encouraged practical benevolence, moral earnest-

---

11. Jorgenson and Solum, *Rölvaag*, p. 17.

ness, promotion of a lay religion, and personal testimony.[12] But its insistence upon conversion and a life of intense religious emotion, combined with the background of inhospitable natural forces in Norway, led frequently to religious melancholy. Arne Garborg's novel *Peace* is a convincing account of the desperate struggle of a morbidly pietistic Norwegian for the assurance that he is saved. The title is ironic, for peace is the one thing he never enjoys.

> He felt always as if he had done some evil—as if he had something to be afraid of. He never felt secure; he could never sit down in comfort—not even in his own house; even if he seemed to be gay in merry company or eager in heated discussions, remorse lay and gnawed within his breast; he was never glad through and through.[13]

Though Haugeanism as an active movement died out in Norway in the 1820s, its teachings continued to influence the religious thinking of many Norwegians into the twentieth century. Rölvaag's later work among Lutherans in America, some of whom held fanatically narrow views and insisted upon stern austerity of living, confirmed his youthful abhorrence of an autocratic church. He disliked the emphasis upon denial, sin, and the ugliness of an evil world existing only to try man's faith. In his novels he frequently suggests the ideal clergyman: a vigorous leader of his people, committed to preserving their cultural integrity and guiding them toward self-knowledge and self-respect.

As a boy Rölvaag felt keen sympathy with humankind; his heart was easily moved to pity and love those who suffered. In the autobiography he writes of a childhood experience which affected him deeply. Among their neighbors was a woman bearing a secret sorrow in her heart—a recluse, known to be "a bit queer," although she was always kind to him. One day she came in great

---

12. The following discussion of pietism as it affected Haugeanism is based upon "Pietism," *The New Schaff-Herzog Encyclopedia of Religious Knowledge*, ed. Samuel Macauley Jackson, vol. 9 (New York: Funk and Wagnalls Co., 1911), pp. 53–67.

13. Arne Garborg, *Peace*, trans. Phillips Dean Carleton (New York: W. W. Norton and Company, 1929), p. 7.

*13*

distress and asked to borrow their boat to make a trip to a nearby hamlet. On her return she left without saying good-by, but he saw her take a loose piece of rope from the boat's prow. Months went by without anyone's seeing her. Then one day when the boy was trolling outside the cove with an old fisherman they came upon something bobbing up and down in the water. It was the body of the woman with the rope still tied around her neck, though the stone had come loose. Even more shocking to the boy than this gruesome discovery was the old fisherman's reaction: practical and matter-of-fact, he simply anchored the body there to be picked up on their way back. Later Rölvaag was troubled by the argument over whether the body should be buried in consecrated ground or outside the wall of the cemetery. "I remember, too," he writes, "how incensed I was over the injustice. Well, she was finally permitted to come inside the fence of the cemetery, but she was buried in a corner all by herself. On the way to and from school I saw her lonely grave every day."

In spite of its dogmatism, the Norwegian state church generally recognized the needs of the people and administered them compassionately. Björnson describes the important place the Lutheran church holds in the heart of the Norwegian peasant:

> [He] sees it standing apart, lonely and sanctified. . . . It is the only house in the valley which he has thought worthy of adornment; its very steeple to him looks higher than it really is. . . . In those silent valleys the church speaks yet a language of its own to every listener, according as the eye that beholds it is young or old. Much may rise up between the church and the grown man, but nothing will rise above it. Awe awakening and perfect, it stands before the young to be received in confirmation; it raises a finger, as it were, half threatening, half beckoning, to the young man leading the maiden to the altar; strong and upright it towers amid the cares of manhood; restful and tender it looks upon the old man's finished toil.[14]

---

14. Björnstjerne Björnson, *Sunny Hill: A Norwegian Idyll* (New York: The Macmillan Company, 1932), pp. 19–20.

## Roots in the Homeland

The religious atmosphere of Rölvaag's home seems not to have been predominantly gloomy—the mother was too good-natured and loving to have permitted that—but certainly it was a sober household. In *The Boat of Longing* the description of Nils Vaag's boyhood home (in reality Rölvaag's) includes mention of a thorn-crowned head of Christ hanging on the wall of the main room. If such a picture hung on the wall of the cottage at Dönna, it would reflect the father's darker temperament. It is difficult to form a clear picture of Rölvaag's parents because he left little record of his boyhood years;[15] however, they do appear as Anna and Jo in *The Boat of Longing* and Rölvaag speaks of them briefly in the autobiographical fragment.

The father's letters to his son in America almost always revealed resignation and disappointment. Like Jo in *The Boat of Longing*, he looked upon the boy's emigration as a personal tragedy and felt that as a consequence his own life would soon be over; yet he welcomed his son back to Norway three times, living until 1931, the year of Rölvaag's death. A letter written in 1905 suggests both the somber religiosity of the home in Norway and the inexpressible love the father bore the son he could not understand:

Rölvaag, March 5, 1905

Dear Ole,

Yesterday I received from your bother Andreas your letter written to him. Yes, it is a real joy to hear from you. That it was not sent to me personally does not matter so much as long as I can see that all goes well with you, and that you have hopes of going forward and reaching your goal. If your thoughts and plans are in agreement with God's plan, then all will be well and you can cheerfully and surely go forward.

---

15. An excellent brief article about Rölvaag as a boy by his childhood companion John Heitmann has been referred to earlier. Mrs. Rölvaag writes that the "vivid descriptions of both Father and Mother Rölvaag are very good and, as far as I know from hearsay, accurate" (Mrs. Rölvaag to the author, November 27, 1957). Heitmann's home was on the eastern coast of Dönna, which is quite fertile; his general description of the island does not apply to the barren, rocky northwestern coastal section where Rölvaag lived.

I see from your letter that you are engaged. To that there is nothing for me to say. You have both my and your mother's blessing.

O, that it may be a Paradise and not a Hell; then this event in your life shall be a step in the shining stairway that carries us upward to our Father's House.

Well, now, I can say that just about all of mine have left me, and my last days are not so bright. But we must put our faith in Him who has said: "Even to your old age I am He, and to gray hairs I will carry you. I have made, and I will bear; I will carry and will save (Isaiah 46:4)." Resting upon such a promise, I have no reason to complain.

I have a deep desire to meet you again before I am gathered to my fathers, but for that there is perhaps no hope. Should you ever return to these familiar places, then stand trustingly on my dust and be assured you have my blessing. A heartfelt "thank you" for all the days you spent in your childhood home.

I must close for this time with a friendly greeting from me and your mother and from us all.

P. Jakobsen Rölvaag[16]

Such letters filled Rölvaag with longing for home. He understood the loneliness of his aging parents and felt responsible for it. In just this situation—the separation of loved ones and the emigrant's renunciation of home—Rölvaag found a truth often overlooked in the record of the great settlement upon the American prairie. The cost of emigration in human suffering he realized profoundly, insisting upon loyalty to native culture and tradition to lessen the shock of transplantation. Writing to his fiancée, Rölvaag could not hide the depression induced by his father's letter:

I was on the point of crying when reading it. The tone is so distinctly sad. They are now just about alone. All of us except my youngest bother have left them. They must feel lonely too. Very likely I am the one most keenly lost. I was Ma's own boy.

---

16. This letter, written in Nordland dialect in antiquated spelling, was translated by Mrs. O. E. Rölvaag.

My brother wrote me some time ago saying that whenever they received a letter from me, then Mother would take it and go out in the kitchen and read it over and over again and cry. These things make me very sad sometimes; almost feel like crying. My heart is aching so to see them once more in this life; and I shall do all in my power to do so. You see neither Father nor Mother was willing that I should go to this country. Somehow I felt that here I was to find my beautiful princess and happiness. [. . .] And God be praised! My feelings did not deceive me. [. . .] Of course, I have many dark and stormy days; yet I am so strangely happy in your love. The worst is when I get the letters from the old country. Then I feel like isolating myself from the world and thinking only of home and my childhood.[17]

According to Rölvaag's wife, who never met his parents but formed an impression of them from the remarks of her husband and others, they were humble and deeply religious people, pietistic only in the sense that their religion was a vividly personal matter without trace of sanctimony. The father especially was somber, partly because of the forbidding natural environment. "He was stubborn in his ways," Mrs. Rölvaag writes, "perhaps brusque and intolerant to some degree, but good to the family as far as his means allowed." The mother was a warmhearted and sensitive woman who sympathized with the boy; it was to her that he turned for understanding and encouragement. "Rölvaag often said that she was the best woman he had ever known," Mrs. Rölvaag continues. "He loved her deeply. Kind, understanding, calm by nature, she supplemented her husband in a worthy way. All who remembered and mentioned Mother Rölvaag when I visited Norway spoke of her as an unusually good woman."[18] She was tempermentally much like Beret Holm in *Giants in the Earth*, relying on the "long-established social and religious order about her. Emptiness would kill her. She was not the sort who could be a

---

17. Rölvaag to Jennie Berdahl, April 2, 1905.
18. Mrs. Rölvaag to the author, October 16, 1957.

blazer of new trails."[19] Her son's decision to emigrate came as a profound shock, but her love for him enabled her to wish him well with quiet heroism. The reliance upon established order was no less strong in the father, who could never understand his son's need to break out of the confines of the fisherman's life in Nordland.

Rölvaag was happy and carefree, according to his own report in the autobiography, until he was seven years old; then a shadow crossed his life—school. The trouble was that he could not—perhaps did not want to—learn to read. He hated his ABC book increasingly as he was "coaxed and beaten" into his studies. His father always considered him duller than his brothers, the black sheep scholastically, and Rölvaag remembered that "when Father tried to teach me, he soon lost patience and boxed my ears, which made me cry; the crying only blurred my sight, making reading impossible."

In his introduction to *Giants in the Earth,* Lincoln Colcord exaggerates Rölvaag's slowness in learning so that the picture which emerges is almost that of an untutored genius. He writes that "his case as a child seemed hopeless—he could not learn." And later that Ole's schooling ended "at the age of fourteen, when his father finally told him that he was not worth educating."[20] On another occasion Colcord refers to Rölvaag's uncle in South Dakota, who at first refused to send him money for passage to America, "doubtlessly influenced by Rölvaag's family reputation [as a dullard]."[21] Again, referring to Rölvaag's decision to enter preparatory school at Canton, South Dakota, Colcord calls going to school "the lesser of two evils," the other being farming. He was still cowed, writes Colcord, by his father's verdict which ruled his life: the pronouncement "that he was not worth educating."

Mrs. Rölvaag notes that her husband spoke of having been an

---

19. Jorgenson and Solum, *Rölvaag,* p. 18.

20. Lincoln Colcord, Introduction to *Giants in the Earth,* by O. E. Rölvaag (New York: Harper and Brothers Publishers, 1927), p. xiii.

21. Ibid., p. xv.

average child in school, who hated to study and worst of all to memorize. He may have been lazy and rebellious, but he had adequate capacity for learning. In those days a student had to recite Bible stories word for word and, according to Mrs. Rölvaag, "This he could not (maybe would not) do! He knew the stories well, and had he been allowed to tell them in his own words in his own expressive dialect, I'm sure those Biblical characters would have come alive." She recalls that he told her of "hiding his catechism one time and helping his mother hunt for it. The mother, sympathetic, knew her boy, spoke kindly to him, and the book was found."[22]

It is also worth noting that although Rölvaag's father was stern and exacting, he did not take the boy out of school because he was not worth educating but because he had finished the work offered at that school. Elementary training usually ended wth confirmation, at which time a boy, especially the son of a poor fisherman, was expected to go to work. Mrs. Rölvaag's letter continues: "Getting even that meager education was quite a struggle. Beginning at the age of eight, the Rölvaag children had seven miles to trudge every morning over a rocky path—fourteen miles per day! I don't wonder, as he said, that he often fell asleep over his book instead of memorizing the lesson."

Though the boy may have been unfit for school, he was nevertheless developing into a poet. In his mind, the autobiography informs us, "dwelt a wonderland of unknown seas and uncharted lands, all mystery-filled. Over the seas I ruled—I alone; over these unknown lands I was king." And school was not all misery; during the long walks in spring and fall terms he came to know his classmates and to share exciting adventures with them. "For then we acquired knowledge, not indeed out of books but from life. How we loved and how passionately we fought!" John Heitmann reports that among his schoolmates, Ole "was considered a scrapper who

---

22. Mrs. Rölvaag to the author, October 16, 1957.

sought rather than tried to avoid a fight, and . . . was lighthearted, frolicsome, and all alive."[23]

When the seven years of common school were over and the boy had been confirmed, he was ready to go to sea. Though his education had been principally religious, he had avidly read books from the parish library in the Heitmann home, sixteen miles away, to which he and his brother Johan frequently tramped in their wooden shoes over marsh, moor, and rocky ridge. They brought home with them in translation the novels of Scott, Cooper, Marryat, Dickens, and Bulwer-Lytton; they also read the novels of the German and Danish romanticists as well as those of their own countrymen, particularly Björnson and Lie.

The tremendous literary activity of the nineteenth century in Norway must be recognized as one of the forces which shaped Rölvaag's art. In the 1830s two opposing trends which persisted throughout the century were given expression by Henrik Wergeland and Johan Welhaven.[24] Wergeland, a poet of exuberant romantic genius, looking back upon the barren decades of Norwegian literature, believed confidently that his country was about to enter a period of maturity promised by an awakening self-consciousness. Extolling the personality of self and nation, he insisted upon freedom and artistic independence and ridiculed the idea that Norway must forever be dependent upon Danish culture, though she had been in the past and though the two countries shared Danish as the official written language. In keeping with European romantic tendencies, Wergeland believed that to understand nature, or to be in harmony with nature, was to know God.

Welhaven, on the other hand, saw liberty as personal and internal, and he represented classical restraint as opposed to Wergeland's romantic ebullience. While Wergeland was passionately

23. Heitmann, "Rölvaag," p. 156.

24. The following discussion of the Norwegian patriot movement and its antecedents is based principally upon Harald Beyer, *A History of Norwegian Literature,* trans. and ed. Einar Haugen (New York: New York University Press, 1956), pp. 117–53.

interested in social reform and in education as a means of elevating the peasant politically and intellectually, Welhaven believed in individual cultivation and appealed to Denmark for continued direction. These two leaders attracted followers, the "patriots" of Wergeland and the "Danophiles" of Welhaven.

By the middle of the nineteenth century a flourishing interest in things Norwegian was evident in ballads, folk tales, dialects, and national themes. All of the arts were marked by deliberate exploitation of a typically Norwegian character. Harald Beyer observes that this newly awakened enthusiasm, which resulted from the patriot movement of Wergeland as well as similar romantic movements in other countries, "was so overwhelming that it has become common to refer to the period as the national 'debut' or 'awakening.' "[25]

The stimulus of the Grimm brothers' collection of fairy tales in Germany led to the collection and publication in the 1840s of a vast amount of folk material, both musical and literary. The most famous work is the two-volume *Norwegian Folk Tales* (1841–44) by Peter Christen Asbjörnsen and Jörgen Engebretsen Moe, an attempt to preserve the Norwegian "folk soul." (The poet in Rölvaag's *The Boat of Longing* has a deep affection for this collection, which he calls the "Book of Wisdom.") Their work contributed significantly to the forming of a new Norwegian prose style, for, as Beyer notes,

> the folk tales demanded a different style from that which had been in vogue in books, one that preserved their character of oral narrative. Asbjörnsen and Moe had to create a new folk tale style, in which the vocabulary admitted new and vivid expressions from the dialects while the sentences were reshaped according to the rules of Norwegian speech.[26]

Rölvaag undoubtedly owed much to the enduring effects of the patriot movement in Norway. He was encouraged to discover the

---

25. Ibid., p. 141.
26. Ibid., p. 142.

beauty of his own musical and picturesque Nordland dialect. His biographers observe that his "literary career exhibits a growing predilection for dialect expressions. . . . He sensed that there was in these folk terms a living reality superior to much in the colorless and stilted language of books."[27] The novels of Björnson and Lie, especially, awakened him to the dignity and individual worth of Norway's country folk and the charm of their plain lives.

Rölvaag was not yet sixteen years old when he went to sea for the first time in January, 1892, in the boat of Beiermann, his old schoolmaster. The craft was one of a fleet headed north for the Lofoten Islands. The boy counted as half a man in the profit-sharing venture. In 1893 he sailed again, experiencing during the winter a furious storm which nearly destroyed boat and crew. The men saved themselves by rowing their stricken vessel to shore, where they collapsed in exhaustion. Jorgenson and Solum suggest that this prolonged exposure and exertion may have permanently damaged his body and caused the bronchial and heart disturbances that plagued him till his death. As a boy he had not been strong; primitive living conditions were not conducive to good health, and often food was short. When it was plentiful he gorged himself, but still, as he reports in the autobiography, "I didn't grow any; the trouble in my chest would not leave me; and sometimes I spit blood, which fact I never mentioned to Mother." He thought enviously of his two great-uncles, who were almost legendary figures because of their prodigious strength. One of them was seen to throw a man over a rocky ledge and out into the harbor, an incident Rölvaag has modified for use in three of his novels—*Letters from America, The Boat of Longing,* and *Giants in the Earth.*

After the memorable winter of 1893, Rölvaag began to think seriously of emigrating to America, but the opportunity did not come immediately. He sailed with the fleet again during the winters of 1894, 1895, and 1896, and—a tribute to his superior seamanship— was offered command of his own boat if he would return. The sea

---

27. Jorgenson and Solum, *Rölvaag*, p. 92.

itself must have contributed to his increasing restlessness; westward from Dönna lay the heaving Atlantic, always in motion, always drawing his thoughts away from the bleak life of the Nordland fisherman toward the promise of a brighter life in the New World.

In the summer of 1896, when the young man was twenty years old, his uncle in South Dakota was able to lend him money for passage. Undoubtedly, Rölvaag recognized the lack of economic and educational opportunity facing him at home and longed to get out into the world to prove his mettle, perhaps especially to his father, who looked to the oldest brother, Johan, as the promise of the family. To the Norwegian familiar with letters from emigrants describing the New World in glowing and frequently inaccurate terms, America was above all a land of boundless opportunity. There one could become anything he desired to be—even a writer, if that was his greatest wish. When Rölvaag left Dönna in July, 1896, it was with a promise to himself that he would soon return. A month later he was in New York City with an American dime and a Norwegian copper piece in his pocket. Like the *askeladd* of the Norwegian fairy tale, he had set forth to discover the mystery of the land across the sea and to win for himself the Castle of Soria Moria.

# THE QUEST FOR IDENTITY
## IN AMERICA

*F*rom the day Rölvaag left Dönna in July of 1896 until January of 1901, he kept a diary, which might well be called his first book. The earliest entries record his depression and loneliness:

> At last I am on my way! I had no idea it would be so hard to leave Mother. Not only Mother—everything—the girl I love so dearly. I thought my heart would surely break. [. . .] I'm going out into the world to seek my fortune and happiness, though happiness can be found only where my sweetheart lives. I'm not even sure I can call her my girl. She is a flirt, but at any rate she was mine before I left (July 29, 1896).[1]

The flourish about the girl does not obscure the real reason for his heavy spirits: separation from homeland and family, especially his mother, whom he missed most of all. Having arrived by boat in Trondheim, Rölvaag wrote:

> Oh, dear Lord, how I yearn to be at home again! This strange longing that has made me ill many a time has again overpow-

---

1. The pocket diary is a small book with heavy cardboard covers and a leather spine. The last entry was made January 6, 1901; after that date apparently Rölvaag was more at home in America and felt less need to express his moods. The diary is not a day-by-day record of events; it served as an outlet for the occasional outpourings of a lonely young immigrant who sometimes experienced bitter disappointments. The moods it reveals do not give a complete picture of Rölvaag's personality. Throughout his life he was a man of emotional extremes, either "up in the clouds or down in the depths. It took so very little to lift his spirits up, and just as little could bring him to the verge of despair. The diary does bring that out to some extent" (Mrs. Rölvaag to the author, February 5, 1958). The translation is based upon one made by Mrs. Rölvaag. Dates are given wherever they appear in the diary.

ered me. I suppose every human being can have such yearnings except that they will be stronger or weaker according to the nature and character of the individual. How I wish it were time to leave this place! If I could travel constantly, that would be better (July 31, 1896).

The following day he visited historical spots in the ancient city, but the loneliness persisted:

It is Saturday evening. I happened to meet an old childhood friend here in Trondheim where I am at present on my way to America. Since life here has been quite dreary, this was wonderful good luck for me. As he is well acquainted, he could take me around and furnish considerable diversion. We first visited the Cathedral, a noble work of art from ancient as well as modern times. It is one of the great sights of the country that I had often wished to see, and I certainly felt repaid for the two hours spent there. Then we went on to several other places, which would have been pleasant enough except for that nagging longing for home. Ah, could I have come home to Mother this evening, then—yes, then—I would certainly be happy. No, I suppose even then something would be lacking. I might be content for a while but surely only for a very short time. The great demands the soul makes [. . .] on the body can never be satisfied so long as man does not belong to God. [. . .] Yes, it is strange how strong this yearning for something better may become (August 1, 1896).

Rölvaag's destination was Christiania (renamed Oslo in 1925), where he would board a ship for America. On his last day in Trondheim his small store of food was gone and he was penniless:

How it will go with me, the dear Lord alone knows. [. . .] Nothing else for me to do but to go to the pawn shop and there borrow a few crowns on my watch. God knows it will be sad to part with my dear watch that carries with it so many precious memories, but necessity drives me to it.

By the time he arrived in Tynset the money was spent, but fortunately he had already bought his ticket through to Christiania:

I have now reached this place [. . .]after traveling an entire day by train. How I shall fare hereafter I do not know. I have lodging here at Tönset [now Tynset] and share a room with a Jew and a fellow from Lofot, both jolly men who will be my companions all the way to Christiania. I lack nothing and should have been well content if only I could have had a talk with Mother. God alone knows if I shall ever see her again (August 4, 1896).

In Christiania he confirmed arrangements to sail the next day, determined to carry out his plan in spite of anxiety about the future. To a young man of twenty who had never been away from home except for the months as a fisherman, the sea between Dönna and the magic land to the west seemed an illimitable expanse. The night before sailing he wrote in his diary:

Now I have arrived in Christiania, and the S. S. Norge leaves here tomorrow at one o'clock in the afternoon. Everything has gone well so far. Only the dear Lord, who rules and guides all for the best for us poor mortals, can know how it will be with me over there in another part of the world. The worst of all is that I have only one and a half dollars in money, and whether or not I can get along on that I do not know. Oh, that I might have reached home this evening to be with Mother, and then with another; but I love them too dearly and because of that I may be denied ever seeing them again. [. . .] I am too tired to write more this evening and with this, I close my notes from Norway. Next time I write I shall likely be in New York. Goodnight then, my dear old Fatherland. It may be the last time I shall rest my weary body in your loving arms. But I shall say with Björnstjerne Björnson:

"I believe that one day I shall reach the goal
Far, far beyond the high mountains!"

Aboard ship he soon tired of his inactivity and found diversion in studying the weather with the eye of a seasoned fisherman:

After traveling four days and four nights, I shall try again to write a few words, imperfect though they be. The weather up to now has been fine, but there seems to be a change from

27

clear sky to fog and rain with signs of a rising wind and storm. People are beginning to be sea-sick. If this develops into a real storm, I'm afraid there will be a bad time on board, especially in the women's cabins. The weather was really fine when we passed the Shetland Islands with only a slight wind and a fairly calm sea; yet many became very sick. I can well imagine what it will be like in case of a real storm. There are two ladies in the cabin farthest aft for whose sakes I should like to see a regular storm (August 10, 1896).

Two days later he wrote:

My wish was not granted. There was no storm, which was best for the many, but how I should have enjoyed seeing the great ocean in a mighty uproar! As a Norwegian fisherman I have many a time been at sea in a storm, but to behold this great Atlantic in a furious rage—that I should like to experience (August 12, 1896).

On August 20 he landed in New York and described his impressions of the city:

Here one can see man's true nature and also view his accomplishments. I felt like a fly that someone had put into a tightly-corked bottle. Of the many immigrants on board ship, only three of us continued our journey together when we left New York in the evening for the Promised Land. It was a magnificent sight for me, coming from the land of the midnight sun, to see the clear, blue, star-lit heaven with a full moon—now in the month of August.

On August 21 he reached Chicago, where he probably stopped a few days before continuing his journey to Elk Point, South Dakota. He noted in his diary his first reaction to the midwestern landscape, which plays such a significant role in his novels: "The countryside was very monotonous, I thought; almost nothing except prairie."

We may turn to Rölvaag's first published novel, *Letters from America* (*Amerika-Breve,* 1912), for a picture of his earliest years in Elk Point, though in the book the central character is named

# The Quest for Identity in America

Per Smevik and the town is called Clarkfield, South Dakota.[2] The book appeared under the pseudonym Paal Mörck because, as Rölvaag later admitted, it is so distinctly autobiographical.[3] Rölvaag, like Per Smevik, was quickly disillusioned about farm life in "New Canaan" and later spoke of his farm years as the "Babylonian captivity." Hours were long and the work was strenuous, even for a former Nordland fisherman. Per Smevik writes in letter 9:

> I do not enjoy life. I go here stomping and mumbling to myself among cows and pigs, thinking of the broad shining waves that roll on the ocean. To ride those waves![4]

In America the restlessness of the boyhood years continued to torment Rölvaag. Learning English was a terrible struggle and like Nils in *The Boat of Longing*, he felt isolated from the strange community. Farm chores offered no challenge, and shortly after his arrival he received news that his sweetheart in Norway was engaged to another man. He turned to the diary again:

> After so long a period has passed, I shall try again to write a little. The learned philosophers say that ideas are developed through expression and also that writing is supposed to cheer one's mind. That is exactly what I need right now.
>
> This gnawing, unsettled feeling within me is terrible. I fear it will drive me mad, and the worst of it is that I know where peace may be found could I but force myself to seek it. Yes, I know, the honorable theologians in their imposing dignity stand there in the pulpits and tell us that peace will be ours if only we *will* it. I say that is a lie. At least, though I *will* to have peace, I lack the determination to wish consistently for the same thing. I really have no will power at all! Today I

---

2. Paal Mörck [O. E. Rölvaag], *Amerika-Breve* (Minneapolis: Augsburg Publishing House, 1912).

3. Draft of an undated letter to Fred Engene. See Jorgenson and Solum, *Rölvaag*, p. 146.

4. Quoted from *Amerika-Breve* in translation by Jorgenson and Solum, *Rölvaag*, p. 39.

may want one thing, tomorrow something entirely different, and that can't be called will power. No, I am like a ship, drifting about rudderless on the roaring sea after a storm. Though the crew should desire to sail in a certain direction, what could they accomplish with their *wills? Nothing.* They are absolutely in the clutches of the elements. So it is with me: I am abandoned to the mercy of my feelings. I cannot stand this continual drifting about on the sea of feeling. The ship will finally spring a leak and—then—then—sink. The honorable theologians say there is no peace for the unconverted after death. This I cannot believe; anyway, during the period between a person's death and judgment, even an ungodly person must find rest. [. . .] My happiest times were when I sat on Mother's lap and she folded my hands and we prayed to God; or when she sang some of her beautiful hymns for me. Then I had peace, I was happy (March 14, 1898).

The cost of the break from home was great, but Rölvaag paid willingly, confident that some day he would succeed. Yet here he was, cleaning the barn and feeding pigs—chores he never had to do in Norway. The infrequent entries in the diary invariably describe his enervating restlessness:

I should like to know what is to become of me. Shall I continue with the life I am now leading, or shall I ever amount to something more? Not much likelihood of the latter. Struggle a while in the conflict, only to give up in despair? No, it's weak spirits that fall, the strong that conquer. Do I then belong to the weak spirits? Well, it would be interesting to know if those so-called "mighty spirits" could have endured what I have this past year. Though they would not have broken, naturally, they might have bent under the "iron-clad" demands. I am not broken either, only bent.

In moments of confidence he believed his drifting would become purposeful movement toward a worthy goal:

Strange indeed if I shall not one day be permitted to accomplish *something*. I feel within me the stirring of mighty forces, but it is difficult to say whether any of these ambitions will ever be realized. [. . .] This I do know, that if I shall ever amount to anything, it will have to be in some place other than Union County, South Dakota; however, this could be a wonderful field of labor for one who knew how to tackle the problem in the best way. Yes, in truth, a great pioneering work could be done if one were able to remake the spiritless creatures living here into human beings. But that requires genius and much learning and a strong will power, and in the last respect I am lacking.

Rölvaag realized that in order to help transform the spirit of Norwegian-Americans, he first of all must continue his education. But entering high school at his age and with a language handicap was a frightening prospect; he thought briefly of enlisting in the Spanish-American War to escape the tormenting restlessness.

Then suddenly and boldly he applied for admission to Augustana Academy at Canton, South Dakota, a Lutheran preparatory school, enrolling for the winter term about Thanksgiving of 1898:

> At last, I'm at the foot of my ambition's ladder! Will I live long enough to reach the top? If one could but take a peek behind that curious curtain and see the future. I'm certain it is better as it is or there would be even more suicides than there are. I do know, however, that this is the wisest move I've ever undertaken. How glorious it is to mingle with a hundred students! That alone develops and sharpens one's mind. A young man, surrounded by a hundred companions, will naturally try to be the best one.

The three years at Augustana Academy confirmed his dissatisfaction with life around him and reawakened an interest in writing as a career. By the time of his graduation in 1901, Rölvaag had a broad sense, at least, of his mission: to foster in America the finest values of the Norwegian heritage.

During the summers of 1899, 1900, and 1901, he held various jobs to earn money for school: itinerant bookselling (he recounts some of his experiences in *Letters from America*), working in the harvest fields, and selling stereopticons in central Iowa. In his travels he met many Norwegian-Americans whose material success blinded them to the necessity of cultivating their spiritual lives. His diary contains this account of his disappointment:

> Again I have tramped about another day and have met with none except crippled souls. They are dead, dead, living dead! Their highest interests are hogs, cattle, and horses. Like worms they dig in the dust and satisfy themselves with filth. When shall these dirt lovers get enough? Isn't it appalling that a human being, created by God to be an intelligent person and given an immortal soul, can say nothing but, "Give us this day our daily bread"! What will become of such earthworms when they die?
>
> The spiritual life, received from God as the most precious gift, is dead. The sense of beauty with which they might perceive the wonders and glories of nature has been killed by the cold hand of materialism. Hunchbacked, with furtive glance and dragging footstep, they trudge forward. Toward what goal? Yes, to die as they have lived. And when death comes they grab the bedstead with their crippled fingers and try by force to hold it back. As in a nightmare they sense its approach and vainly try to escape. A last struggle for life, and the dwarfed soul gives up its equally dwarfed dwelling. What becomes of such a soul? What can it answer on Judgment Day when the judge asks: "What have you done with the intellect I gave you?"
>
> "With that I have raised hogs."
>
> "Is that all?"
>
> "No, I have also used it to deceive others as much as I could."
>
> "Is that all?"
>
> "No, I have also used it to conceive some means whereby I might be able to prevent all needy persons from enjoying the bounty of life."
>
> A beautiful document to bring forth! Thank God, there are also other people (June 13, 1900).

In the fall of 1901 Rölvaag enrolled at St. Olaf in Northfield, Minnesota, a college operated by Norwegian Lutherans in America, seriously considering preparation for the ministry. One of the most powerful influences of the next four years came from his systematic study of Norwegian literature, particularly the works of Ibsen, Björnson, and Jonas Lie, in the classes of Professor Peter J. Eikeland.[5] Rölvaag responded wholeheartedly to Ibsen's insistence upon the life-integrating ideal. He could say with Brand:

> Be what you are with all your heart,
> And not by pieces and in part.[6]

Fundamental to Ibsen's philosophy is a belief in the individual's call or mission, expressed in the opening words of his early work *Catiline:* "I *must,* I *must,* so bids a voice within / My soul, and I shall follow its commands." He asserts that one's mission demands the sacrifice of personal desires, that the dedicated personality accepts conflict as inevitable. The poet, he insists, must be a propagandist and cannot withdraw into pure estheticism, ignoring his responsibility to others. Falk in *Love's Comedy,* a poet fighting hypocrisy and compromise, expresses Ibsen's own creed:

> My four-walled chamber poetry is done;
> My verse shall live in forest and in field,
> I'll fight under the splendour of the sun;—
> I or the Lie—one of us two must yield.[7]

This view of art Rölvaag also accepted absolutely.

Living with Ibsen's plays, first as student and later as teacher, Rölvaag inevitably sought to discover an ideal large enough to integrate his own personality. He imagined himself uttering Brand's answer to the peasant who warns him he must turn aside from the trackless snowfields or he will be dead before daybreak: "I must go on. . . . A great one gave me charge; I must. . . . His name is God."[8]

The optimism of Björnson was equally attractive to Rölvaag. He shared Björnson's intense love of humanity and faith in progress, particularly as expressed in his peasant tales with their plain, honest

---

5. Throughout their study (particularly on pp. 57 ff.), Jorgenson and Solum frequently point out how Eikeland's interpretation of Ibsen influenced Rölvaag.

6. Henrik Ibsen, *Brand,* trans. C. H. Herford, in *Collected Works of Henrik Ibsen,* ed. William Archer (New York: Charles Scribner's Sons, 1907), p. 23.

7. Henrik Ibsen, *Love's Comedy,* in ibid., p. 405.

8. Ibsen, *Brand,* p. 4.

heroes struggling to become better men. He also admired Björnson's simplicity of style and compression of language, which give his stories a ruggedness suggestive of the Norwegian countryside. Björnson's spirited defense of native Norwegian art inspired Rölvaag to believe that in spite of the poverty of Norwegian immigrant expression in America, the raw material was there, awaiting only the touch of a dedicated artist.

During the student years at St. Olaf, Rölvaag's interest in writing deepened. A few of his early efforts survive today, either in college composition books or in the pages of the St. Olaf College student newspaper, the *Manitou Messenger*. The stories show Björnson's influence, and the essays are sentimentally idealistic.[9] His most important literary work of these college years dates from 1904–1905, when he attempted his first novel, *Nils and Astri*, an immature, moralizing, and melodramatic effort.[10] The novel is in two parts. Part 1, subtitled "The Greenfield Youngsters," which pictures life in a Norwegian-American community, is based largely on Rölvaag's experiences as a parochial school teacher at Bisbee, North Dakota, during the summer of 1904. Nils, a motherless boy of artistic temperament and a lover of the violin like Nils in *The Boat of Longing*, is drawn to the kind teacher, Asmundsen, who appears to be patterned after the teacher in Björnson's *A Happy Boy*. There is an ill-conceived villain, Per Amandus, and a pure and idealistic heroine, Astri Bjarne. In part 2, "The Greenfield Youngsters Grow Up," the chief characters are brought together eight years later. It is noteworthy, as Jorgenson and Solum observe, that in the Norwegian settlement "the question of how much of its racial background ought to be carried over into the new environment not only arises but comes strongly into the foreground in many a discussion."[11]

---

9. For a discussion of these early productions, see Jorgenson and Solum, *Rölvaag*, pp. 58 ff.

10. This unpublished novel, written in Norwegian, is in the Rölvaag Collection.

11. Jorgenson and Solum, *Rölvaag*, p. 77.

## The Quest for Identity in America

During the summers of 1902 and 1903, Rölvaag earned money for college expenses by teaching parochial school in Newcastle, Nebraska. In the summer of 1903, his friendship with Jennie Berdahl, the sister of an Augustana Academy friend, deepened into a love that culminated in their engagement the following year. The next summer he taught again, first at Churchs Ferry and then at Bisbee, North Dakota. His funds were supplemented by earnings at college, where he did custodial work. Plans for the future were taking shape; he joked in a letter to Miss Berdahl about becoming a "good-for-nothing Prof" and said that he intended to return to Norway for a visit after graduation. "You cannot imagine," he wrote, "how I long to see them, and especially, Mother."[12]

At St. Olaf College commencement exercises on June 14, 1905, Rölvaag, who was graduated with honors, delivered an oration called "Individuality." He expressed a growing respect for personality, which he defines as the sum total of the potentialities which God has placed in the soul of each man.[13] His increased understanding of Ibsen led to his insistence upon the uniqueness of each person. In *Brand,* the idealistic preacher is chastized by the Dean for having "striven to express / And emphasize unlikenesses" so that "the Church no longer is the hood / That fits alike on every head." The aim of the church, as of the state, ought to be to insure conformity: "All men to step alike and beat / The selfsame music with their feet." But Brand fights to create a society which exploits human differences rather than encourages conformity. On a broader scale, Rölvaag envisioned a society in which national groups preserve and respect their separate cultural achievements at the same time that they share a common American tradition.

On July 15, 1905, Rölvaag wrote excitedly to Miss Berdahl that he was going to Norway for a year of graduate study at the University of Christiania. For a long time he had dreamed of visiting Dönna during the summmer after graduation, but until now it

---

12. Rölvaag to Jennie Berdahl, April 13, 1904.
13. This commencement address, written in Norwegian, is in the Rölvaag Collection.

seemed impossible. On an impulse he went to President J. N. Kildahl of St. Olaf College and asked to borrow five hundred dollars. Kildahl was pleased to make the loan on behalf of the college and invited him back as a teacher of Norwegian when a position opened, perhaps the following year.

At this time he was twenty-nine years old and had been away from Norway almost ten years. After visiting his fiancée and uncle in South Dakota, Rölvaag bought a ticket (for which he paid fifty-six dollars) from Northfield to Christiania. He left Northfield August 14, 1905, and four days later wrote from aboard ship:

> It is about eleven at night. We are way, way out on the Atlantic. I have been walking the deck since dusk. When I finally turned in my coat was so wet with the spray that I had to change. Haven't had anything on my head all night. Had to feel the sea breeze and the salt water once more.[14]

He also described his activities in New York City on the preceding day. Like Nils in *The Boat of Longing*, Rölvaag was fascinated by the throngs of people and the hidden drama of each life. He visited several churches, including St. Paul's and St. Timothy's, and was surprised to discover many persons kneeling in prayer:

> Noticed especially a young man. He couldn't be past twenty. [. . .] A very fine looking youth he was. He seemed to be in great distress. On his face was written despair. He seemed actually to be wrestling with God in prayer, as Jacob of old. Evidently he was sustaining a great sorrow. That scene made a lasting impression on me. Just imagine the contrast between *that* scene and that outside the church: the endless, madly rushing crowd on Broadway![15]

By September he was settled in Christiania where he found life at the university lonely, the atmosphere and teaching methods unfamiliar:

---

14. Rölvaag to Jennie Berdahl, August 18, 1905.
15. Ibid.

Yes, I was among my own people and so to speak in my own country, but yet I felt so strange. Really, I am a foreigner so far as Norway is concerned. Can't even talk Norwegian. Never realized *before* that I knew so little of the Norwegian language. If anyone had told me before I came to Christiania that I knew so little, I would have felt insulted. And strange I felt toward everything except toward *nature*. That I *can* understand.[16]

But that even his love of nature was tinged with melancholy can be seen in a letter he wrote several weeks later, describing a great pine forest which cast its gloomy spell over him:

One Sunday I was up in the pine forest district called "Nordmarken." It comprises many miles and is perfectly desolate as far as human inhabitants goes. There one can easily get lost, unless he is very careful. [. . .] On an autmun day it is very still in that forest. There is nothing to break the stillness except the sighing. [. . .] That sighing, old as the pine forest, seems to conceal within it all the sorrow and sadness of the ages. And no wonder; for here many a young maiden's soul has cried to the Eternal to heal her sorrow inflicted either by lustful or deceitful love. Here she has snuggled close up to nature's heart —alone with God in the great stillness of the forest. Here, too, many a strange youth with hopes broken, with ambition thwarted has sought consolation. [. . .] The gay [. . .] never come here; they know that the silent forest will rob them of their gaiety.[17]

Rölvaag missed the informality of school life in America but dug into his studies, determined to prove that the "American student," as he referred to himself, was worth noticing. Notebooks preserved from this year bear the subject headings "History of Norwegian Literature," "The Norwegian Language," "Norwegian Folk Lore," "The Sagas," "Norwegian Political History," "Recent

---

16. Rölvaag to Jennie Berdahl, October 15, 1905.
17. Rölvaag to Jennie Berdahl, October 28, 1905.

German History," "Semantics," "Wergeland," "Psychology," and "Philosophy."[18]

In November, 1905, one of Norway's publishing firms, H. Aschehoug and Company (later to undertake the publication of the two volumes which appeared in America as *Giants in the Earth*), rejected the manuscript of his novel, *Nils and Astri.* To Miss Berdahl he wrote the bitter news:

> I want to tell you very frankly, that if you ever had any high hopes of me as an author, or any hopes of me ever becoming an author, then you shall discard such hopes. They have no grounds. I am an ordinarily gifted man; very common indeed. That's all. [. . .] It wasn't the thirst for vainglory which made me try to write. I wanted to do something for the Norwegian Americans on a large scale, and that I thought I could do through my authorship.[19]

During the winter Rölvaag was ill with diphtheria and because of a subsequent bronchial complication was hospitalized for a time. He wrote of his conviction that he had a special mission to perform:

> Many queer things have I thought of while I have been sick. One night I couldn't go to sleep. I began to think of how bad it would be if I should die. I had so many things I wanted to do first—things I must do. [. . .] Yet, it wasn't because I was afraid of death, but because so many things would be undone that nobody else but I could do.[20]

In spite of physical weakness and depression, he returned to his classes upon release from the hospital. The evaluation of his year's work depended upon a final examination, which he feared he might

---

18. These subject headings are translated from the Norwegian. For discussions of several of the prominent teachers with whom Rölvaag studied—notably Arne Löchen (psychology), Gerhard Gran (Norwegian literature), and Moltke Moe (Norwegian ballads)—see Jorgenson and Solum, *Rölvaag*, pp. 91 ff.

19. Rölvaag to Jennie Berhahl, November 6, 1905.

20. Rölvaag to Jennie Berdahl, January 23, 1906.

fail. But with spring's coming his enthusiasm returned, and he expressed his love of the Norwegian countryside:

> The surroundings seem to be too strong for the people and the people are suffering because of them. And yet people grown up in such nature can never be really happy any other place in the world. If they come to other countries, the rivers, the mountains, the forests, the fjords, the ocean, the darkness of the long winter, the peculiar light of the short summer night— all these things so peculiar to Norwegian nature will forever have a mystic power over him who dreamt his childhood's dreams here.[21]

Rölvaag took the final examination May 22, 1906, and reported that he received the highest grade attainable.[22] That the Norwegian immigrant had become Americanized is clear from a letter he wrote to Miss Berdahl:

> I am very glad that I stood perfect; not that the standing is worth anything in itself, but I was an American, and the big fellows in Christiania have not much faith in us.[23]

Two weeks after graduation he was back in his boyhood home on Dönna, experiencing the peace he had been seeking:

> What shall I say and what shall I write? I don't know, for I never experienced anything like it [before]. The greatest blessing on earth is a home and the greatest within the home is mother. Can't tell you what I felt when seeing my parents and my sisters and brothers. The feeling was so much unlike anything earthly I have ever experienced. Now I am only floating on love and good things to eat and drink.[24]

While in Nordland Rölvaag gave a speech called "American Social Conditions," expressing disappointment in the life of Norwegian-Americans, the same note of disillusionment heard so dis-

---

21. Rölvaag to Jennie Berdahl, March 29, 1906.

22. Rölvaag received the Candidate of Philosophy degree, which is roughly equivalent to the master's degree, awarded after five years of university work.

23. Rölvaag to Jennie Berdahl, June 6, 1906.

24. Ibid.

tinctly in *Letters from America, Pure Gold,* and *The Boat of Longing:*

> There is emptiness and hollowness in a degree that must surprise every person capable of deep emotions. [. . .] The everyday life is uniform and without nuance. It lacks depth and heartfelt, spontaneous joy. Although the Americans have shown a mechanical ingenuity greater than that of any other people, they have not yet discovered the art of living. Neither the Yankee nor the Norwegian-American has been able to determine the proper relation between earning money and using it in the interest of human wellbeing. [. . .] What an abundance of originality in a small land like Norway! . . . Every little community has its distinctness in language as well as in custom, and every town and farm has individuality.[25]

Rölvaag's return to the grandeur of Norway's landscape was to have a powerful effect upon the coming novels through his vivid realization of man's insignificance against nature. On a mountain-climbing expedition in Sogn later that summer his spirit was depressed, then overwhelmed, and finally exalted by the vast size and agelessness of the Jostedals glacier.

> But as I listened, it seemed as if the glacier itself crept in upon me, penetrated me, sucked my blood. I grew dizzy; I had to lie down. Every second felt as if it would be the last. Yet it was not a sensation as that of a man fainting. It was like becoming extinct. Inch by inch I passed into nothingness. [. . .] I felt as if I were in the presence of a super-human passion.[26]

This idea of nature as capable of annihilating man appears first in *On Forgotten Paths,* but most impressively in *Giants in the Earth,* where "the Great Plain drinks the blood of Christian men." At the moment of his deepest despair, however, Rölvaag discovered life in the midst of desolation; and this is his essential optimism asserting itself. Flowers bloomed beside the vast ice field in which neither bird nor animal dwelt:

---

25. Translated by Jorgenson and Solum, *Rölvaag,* p. 100.
26. Translated by Jorgenson and Solum, ibid., p. 102.

Bluebells! Think of it, bluebells! They grew at the edge of the snow and in fact right in the snow wherever there was a bit of soil in which they might strike root. I was happy to see the bluebells. Life was with me again; I was not alone in the desolation; I was comforted as by the meeting with a friend.[27]

He returned to Northfield in September, 1906, and began teaching in the Norwegian department of St. Olaf Academy, a preparatory school. He was now in a position to write with understanding of life in both Norway and America and began unconsciously to lay the groundwork for his novels. During Christmas vacation of 1907 he visited Jennie Berdahl in Garretson, South Dakota; they planned to be married the following summer. Rölvaag was greatly interested in the pioneering experiences of the Berdahl family:

. . . [Jennie's father] and his brothers had crossed the stretches west of Fillmore County, Minnesota, to be among the early settlers in the lower Sioux valley. The artist who was instinctively building a foundation for the structure he was later to rear found ample opportunity to supplement his own experiences at Elk Point with those of settlers from an earlier day.[28]

On May 17, 1907, Norwegian Independence Day, Rölvaag in an address to a Norwegian-American audience described what men lose when they give up their fatherland for rights in America.[29] The losses, of course, are not material ones. Chief among them is "the intimate spiritual communion between the individual and his people," a communion fostered by common language, customs, and traditions. Rölvaag's belief that it was imperative for Norwegian-Americans to preserve the culture and language of their fathers has often been misunderstood. It is not parochialism that he advocated. He did not want Norwegians to exist in isolation from other Americans; rather he encouraged them to preserve their individuality at the same time that they absorbed the values

---

27. Ibid.
28. Jorgenson and Solum, *Rölvaag*, p. 109.
29. Translated by Jorgenson and Solum, *Rölvaag*, pp. 113–16.

of the new culture. He was convinced, Einar Haugen notes, that unless they retained their cultural identity, they could not make a valuable contribution to American civilization:

> He regretted their rapid rejection of traditions, and admonished them to keep alive the knowledge of their ancestral language and to deepen and increase their familiarity with the Norwegian culture.[30]

In that address Rölvaag spoke also of the Norwegian-American's opportunity to share in three cultures—American, English, and Norwegian—and of the foolish waste in turning one's back upon the riches of one's heritage. If a successful settlement is to be made, the transplanted roots must be carefully nourished. Some of the old soil must be mixed with the new.

During the winter of 1910, Rölvaag helped to found the Society for Norwegian Language and Culture, an organization, primarily of teachers, concerned with preserving Norwegian culture in America and improving the teaching of the Norwegian language.[31] As secretary of the group he learned to know well other men who shared his objectives. Through his enthusiastic letter writing he was instrumental in laying the groundwork for the establishment of similar organizations in later years, most notably the Norwegian-American Historical Association, which came into being October 6, 1925.

Meanwhile, in the summer of 1909, Rölvaag had again submitted the manuscript of his early novel, *Nils and Astri,* this time to the publications board of the United Norwegian Lutheran

---

30. Einar Haugen, "O. E. Rölvaag: Norwegian-American," *Norwegian-American Studies and Records* 7 (1933): 56–57.

31. In 1910 there was almost no organized interest in Norwegian language and literature. Modern Language Association membership in that year was divided into three groups: English, Germanic languages, and Romance languages. A separate Scandinavian section was not formed until 1921. Of the twenty-seven articles appearing in *PMLA* during 1910, only three were in Germanic studies and only one of these in Norwegian. Of the forty-three papers read at the annual meetings that year, only nine were in Germanic studies and only one of these in Norwegian.

Church of America, but they too rejected it. Subsequent efforts to negotiate its publication in Norwegian-American newspapers also failed. Deciding to make a fresh start, early in 1910 he began writing his second novel, *Letters from America,* in which he hoped to dramatize the problem of the immigrant's peculiar relation to the environments of two worlds.

The next few years were relatively uneventful ones during which Rölvaag devoted himself to teaching and writing. In spite of recurring illness, financial struggle, and anxiety about his family in Norway, he was optimistic about his role in the development of his people in America. When he moved into his own home from the college dormitory where he and his wife had been living since their marriage in 1908, he was able to spend even more time writing, and in 1912 Augsburg Publishing House brought out his first book, *Letters from America.* Though its sale was extremely limited, critical response was encouraging, and Rölvaag was finally recognized in the Middle West as the literary representative of his people. He was soon at work on another novel, *On Forgotten Paths* (1914), in which the heroine personifies not only filial devotion but also a return to the ways of the fathers, which have been abandoned by most of the other inhabitants of the immigrant community in which she lives. Though Rölvaag engaged in no major literary activity from 1914 to 1918, he discussed with friends his plans for a novel about pioneer life in which the hero would be a pastor, a cultural as well as spiritual leader of his people, sensitive to their need for good schools and libraries and interested in stimulating creative life.[32]

On June 21, 1916, Rölvaag began his second trip back to Norway. Though his mother had died the previous year, Dönna drew him as powerfully as ever. Writing to his wife he admitted that he wept when he saw Norway's west coast rising out of the sea. At

---

32. According to Mrs. Rölvaag, her husband spoke frequently of his intention to write a novel in which the noble work of the pioneer pastor would be adequately appreciated. "That will be a beautiful book," he would say. Mrs. Rölvaag to the author, November 29, 1957.

home he enjoyed fishing—"the ancient trade of all the Rölvaags"—and visited with his father, brothers, sisters, nieces, and nephews. The trip proved to him beyond any doubt that though his love for the homeland was as strong as ever, he was unmistakably an American. He perceived more clearly than ever before the drama inherent in this dual relationship. Only through appreciation of his heritage could one successfully bridge the gap between two utterly different cultures. As Einar Haugen observes:

> Everything of consequence that he wrote was either a loving delineation or a bitter scourging of his Norwegian people in America. His love of his race established two fixed poles between which his thoughts were forever oscillating: his devotion to the past in Norway, the heritage of his people; and his concern about their future in America, the fate of the Norwegian immigrant.[33]

He returned to St. Olaf as head of the Department of Norwegian in September of 1916, resolved to enhance the Norwegian contribution to American civilization, a goal he felt he could best accomplish in a college like St. Olaf with its avowed interest in Norwegian culture.

During the years following World War I, Rölvaag wrote two novels which explore the dangers facing the immigrant who breaks away from the old world but does not really belong to the new. In *Two Fools* (1920) his principle characters are members of the second generation whose instinct toward family loyalty is subverted into lust for gold. *The Boat of Longing* (1921), strongly autobiographical in parts, is about a young immigrant artist's struggle against the materialism which threatens to undermine his ideals. In writing these two novels, as well as the earlier ones, Rölvaag was laying the groundwork for his masterpiece, *Giants in the Earth*. He now understood clearly his life's mission: to tell the true story of pioneer life on the prairie, revealing the cost as well as the gain of the great land taking.

---

33. Haugen, "O. E. Rölvaag," p. 53.

# 3

# THE
# APPRENTICE NOVELS:
## *letters from america* AND
## *on forgotten paths*

*E*arly in 1910 Rölvaag began writing *Letters from America* to show the immigrant's relation to both his new and old environments, emphasizing his foreignness to people in the homeland as well as in the land of his adoption. According to Theodore C. Blegen, the publishing of letters from America to Norway reached a peak between the years 1836 and 1850, when a series of "America" books, letters, and pamphlets came from Norwegian presses. Typical of these reports—written by Norwegian immigrants, visitors, or even purveyors of hearsay—were Ole Rynning's *True Account of America for the Information and Help of Peasant and Commoner* (1838), which pictured America as a place of refuge for Europe's poverty-stricken masses, and Peter Testman's *Brief Account of the Most Important Experiences during a Sojourn in North America* (1839), which warned Norwegians against supposing that America was truly a land of opportunity.[1]

It was perhaps inevitable that Rölvaag should choose to cast his first novel in the form of "America letters." As a Norwegian whose own decision to emigrate had been influenced by such accounts in Norwegian newspapers, he decided to tell his story of a newcomer's experiences through a series of communications with the family in Norway. The letters represent three periods in Per Smevik's life in America: his first two years in Clarkfield, South

---

1. Theodore C. Blegen, *Norwegian Migration to America: 1825–1860* (Northfield, Minn.: Norwegian-American Historical Association, 1931), pp. 196–213.

Dakota—in reality Elk Point—(fifteen letters); his experiences as a student (four letters); and his experiences as a teacher of parochial school (four letters). The last group includes observations on the pettiness of factions in the Norwegian Lutheran Church of America and criticism of their failure to minister to the needs of the people. *Letters from America (Amerika-Breve,* 1912) was published pseudonymously by Augsburg Publishing House, official publishing agency for the Norwegian Lutheran Church of America, after having been rejected by Aschehoug Publishing Company in Christiania. Rölvaag's brother Johan wrote from Norway to tell him that it had been read aloud at home, mentioning his mother's enthusiasm and his father's apparent indifference; however, in an article about the Rölvaag family, Heitmann reveals that in later years, the father admitted being greatly pleased by his son's attainments, though he seemed incapable of telling him so.[2] The book had an extremely limited circulation, chiefly among Norwegian-speaking members of the Lutheran church, but the reviews were favorable. And when Rölvaag's authorship was revealed, he attracted considerable attention among his countrymen in America.

Only in the broadest sense can *Letters from America* be called a novel; the twenty-three communications are loosely related, and only the main character is clearly delineated. Even he emerges as a type of the enterprising newcomer rather than as a distinct personality like Nils Vaag, the Norwegian immigrant in Rölvaag's later novel *The Boat of Longing.* Many of the episodes are merely jokes, the laughter arising from misunderstandings caused by language difficulties and different customs. Suggestions are to be found, certainly, of Rölvaag's interest in the failure of Norwegians in America to create a worthy culture; and like the young and disillusioned Knut Hamsun, Rölvaag expressed his disappointment in the materialism of Americans, among whom he found a preponderance of money-

---

2. Heitmann, "Rölvaag," p. 156.

grubbers.[3] Yet, it is not the inner, but the outer life which concerns him chiefly.[4]

The letters are purported to be written by Per Smevik to his father and brother in Norway, who later join him in America; and are collected for publication by a friend of the father, Paal Mörck. How closely the episodes described in the letters parallel Rölvaag's own experiences can be seen by a comparison of an actual letter with a summary of one of the literary letters. In letter 23 Rölvaag records the following incident: One evening during the summer Per Smevik teaches parochial school, a stranger asks him to preach a sermon at the funeral of his little boy. He lives twenty miles out in the country and is unable to find a minister. Per agrees reluctantly and is picked up the next afternoon by the man's neighbor. He learns from the driver that the bereaved father is an infidel and has lost three sons, none of whom had been baptized. When Per arrives he sees a black coffin in the center of the tiny one-room hut, the sorrowing parents nearby. He had been determined to preach the law, but the mother's anguish softens his heart and instead he preaches God's love. Never before has he talked so fervently; he seems to be an instrument in the hand of God.

Here is the actual letter, written July 4, 1904:

> I am now at Churchs Ferry. That month at Bisbee was the hardest term of school I ever had. I did not want to tell you about it in my last letter lest you should be anxious. I had

---

3. Though Hamsun wrote no "America letters," he did record his unfavorable impressions of America in *Of American Culture (Fra det Moderne Amerikas Aandsliv,* 1899), a caustic and often witty attack upon America's national conceit, materialism, and cultural sterility. Several of the stories in the collections *Copsewood (Kratskog,* 1903) and *The Struggle of Life (Stridende Liv,* 1905) reflect the same attitudes.

4. The first English translation of *Amerika-Breve* was published by the Dillon Press of Minneapolis in 1971. See also the Ph.D. dissertation by Robert Stevens, "Ole Edvart Rölvaag: A Critical Study of His Norwegian-American Novels" (University of Illinois, 1955), pp. 23–43 and pp. 213–36, for detailed summaries of each of the twenty-three letters and for translations of several extracts. Jorgenson and Solum, too, have quoted generously from the book in their lengthy discussion.

fifteen, sixteen, and seventeen year old town boys, genuine toughs. It was no easy task to control them and still less easy was it to teach them religion. But it went all right. I left Bisbee last Saturday. Thursday night there came a man to me and wanted me to preach a funeral sermon over his two year old boy. There was no preacher to get and the man seemed sorrowful. What could I do? I am just a little bit too good-hearted. So I promised that I would go with him the next afternoon if he would come and get me. The next day at two a man came after me and I had to go. It was only seventeen miles out in the country! From my talk with the driver I began to fear that the little boy was not baptized. I was in an awful pinch. At last we came to the place—one of the dirtiest and filthiest I ever saw. It was very sad! It was as I feared; the boy was not baptized. Oh! the sorrow and anguish of that mother. That hour I prayed very fervently that my own dear little wife should be spared such scenes. I was determined to preach the law to those people and tell them about their crime against their boy; but I said very little about the law. I talked about *God as love, God as a father,* and never before have I talked as I did that hour and I doubt that I ever shall again.[5]

The element of the midwestern landscape associated inseparably with Rölvaag is the prairie. In *Letters from America* Per sets down his first impressions:

Flat as our floor at home. Not a house to be seen. Nothing but endless fields and meadows. Some fields were recently plowed, some were just harvested. Shocks of grain stood in interminable rows. All was flat and without end. [. . .] Now for the first time I became aware of the evening itself; it was a living thing all around me—an eternal humming and buzzing everywhere. [. . .] It seemed to emanate from every blade of grass, every stalk or stem, every speck of dust around me. My courage returned; I even whistled a soft melody.[6]

Already evident in this early work is Rölvaag's characteristic concept of the prairie as a living presence, acquiring personality in

---

5. Rölvaag to Jennie Berdahl, July 4, 1904.

6. Quoted from letter 1, translated by Jorgenson and Solum, *Rölvaag*, p. 34.

his later novels as a spirit either beneficent or evil, capable of destroying man's soul and body. In his next book, *On Forgotten Paths,* the prairie reflects this dual personality, not always evil and destructive, but inevitably more powerful than any human being who proclaims his superiority over natural forces.

*On Forgotten Paths (Paa Glemte Veie,* 1914) is Rölvaag's first novel defining the need to conserve the ways of the fathers, not only because they are the right ways but also because they are the familiar ways that can bridge the gap between two completely different cultures.[7] In a variation of the age-old story of a peasant who loses his soul in quest of riches, the prairie evokes in man a greed which eventually destroys him, an idea Rölvaag explores with much greater success in his next novel, *Two Fools.*

In later years Rölvaag believed that *On Forgotten Paths* was not a true child of his spirit, recognizing that he had allowed applied theology to crowd out human passions and to twist the characters into mere pawns. Among the novel's other serious flaws are its sentimentality and tractarian flavor, its melodramatic flourishes, and its stilted dialogue.

Yet the novel has several virtues which deserve attention. It conveys a sense of the power of both Chris Larsen and the prairie, and of the inevitable tension between them as Chris's antagonism grows, resulting in his defeat. Though the novel fails as a religious document, it is modestly successful as a record of nature's invincible superiority over man. There are frequent suggestions of Rölvaag's mature and characteristic style: a terseness of language and a starkness in descriptive and narrative passages, suggesting the elemental quality of man's struggle against nature. Also striking

---

7. Paal Mörck [O. E. Rölvaag], *Paa Glemte Veie* (Minneapolis: Augsburg Publishing House, 1914). An English translation, which remains unpublished, was made about 1918 by Mrs. C. F. Nickerson, then a student of Rölvaag at St. Olaf College. Mrs. Nickerson has kindly permitted me to read the manuscript, which carries Rölvaag's comments and suggestions for revision in his own handwriting. Quotations in this discussion are my adaptations of Mrs. Nickerson's literal translation, unless otherwise indicated.

is his growing use of contrast as he brings together the incompatible Magdalene and Chris or portrays the varying moods of the prairie.

Christian Larsen is a Norwegian-American of the second generation, his wife a newcomer; their story is about the spiritual rather than physical dangers which settlers face upon the prairie. Larsen, the richest man in the Clarkfield settlement (the scene also of *Letters from America*), has made a fortune in farming and land speculation. He is a pioneer of tremendous physical energy—ruthless, selfish, apparently the child of fortune. The great disappointment of his life is his wife, whom he does not love. Complete opposites in temperament, they were married shortly after she came from Norway. What brought them together they themselves do not know, though the reader understands readily that Chris's practical nature would operate in the matter of selecting a wife much as it operated in selecting cattle.

As a child Chris knew poverty and continual friction between his parents and grew up with one thought in mind: to conquer the prairie, which he looks upon as his chief adversary. Jorgenson and Solum do not emphasize sufficiently his complete selfishness:

> He is himself a splendid type of pioneer, strong of frame and intense with physical energy. His endurance seems unlimited. In addition he is shrewd and resolute. He lacks one thing, namely, warmth, or sentiment. . . . But even in this respect, Larsen is richer than he at first appears to be. His grief over the death of his favorite child, the young son, is as profound as any that a normal human being could sustain.[8]

But in the novel there is no sign whatever that the grief over his son's death stems from sympathy and tenderness; rather he is angry because he has lost his most treasured possession, the heir to the vast kingdom on earth which Chris will possess when he has subdued the prairie. This boy was to have become more powerful and shrewd than any of his fellows.

---

8. Jorgenson and Solum, *Rölvaag*, p. 200.

The chief joy Chris experiences is the malicious satisfaction of destroying his enemies. And if he is happy as he plows the rich, black loam it is in anticipation of the riches to be wrested from the "great brooding troll" who forever mocks him. One of the admirable aspects of this early novel is Rölvaag's conception of the utter meanness of spirit in Chris, of the arrogance and cruelty of a man who lives absolutely for himself.

Magdalene, on the other hand, is a delicate being for whom life with Chris is an ordeal:

> She came to think of her journey to America as her life's greatest sin, from which flowed all other evils. It was to be expected that with her the memories of her homeland did not fade with the years; no, they grew, took on fantastic forms. [. . .] In her mind it remained firmly fixed that all which was good was over there and all which was cold and evil and depressing belonged to the prairie. Both her parents and her grandparents were Haugeaners, and as far back as she could remember, she had heard more about the life beyond than about this earthly life.

The unhappy woman finds solace in her dreams of Norway in which home and the hereafter are strangely mingled.

These two characters strongly suggest Per Hansa and Beret Holm in *Giants in the Earth.* Rölvaag attempts to show in their relationship the cost of the land taking in terms of spiritual stress, asserting the impossibility of surviving dislocation without the support of tradition and community. The immigrant who cannot meet the demands upon him is destroyed—sometimes physically, sometimes spiritually. Magdalene's retreat is a form of destruction as is Chris's almost paranoid determination to subdue the prairie. Jorgenson and Solum point out that Rölvaag tended to think of the pioneers in two wholly different groups:

> the born adventurers and builders of kingdoms, who are given the heroic role even though they do not always elicit our full sympathy; and the frail sensitive natures, who, having no ade-

quate means of protection in the bitter struggle with the prairie, become the tragic figures.⁹

Two children are born to Chris and Magdalene, a daughter and a son. The father shows no interest in the girl, feeling that "he had been cheated in some inexplicable manner—it should have been a boy." But the son becomes the new center of his life. When the baby is a month old, Magdalene slips and falls while carrying him. The distraught father holds the injured child in his arms long into the night, and when it finally dies, walks angrily out of the house.

> He went straight to his workshop in the machine shed and began to nail together a coffin. When it was finished, he carried it to the house and placed the boy in it; not a word passed his lips; the wife was also silent. Then he took the coffin in his arms and went out. On the east side of the house lay a gentle slope where a solitary cottonwood grew; by that tree he buried his son. When he had filled the grave he straightened himself to his full height, looked toward the heavens, where the day was breaking, and cursed bitterly: "From this day forward, You need not meddle in my affairs again!"

After the death of the boy, life with Magdalene becomes unbearable and Chris wants to send her and the girl back to Norway. It can all be arranged decently, he explains, so there will be no talk of divorce. She will simply go on an extended visit. Magdalene will not agree to a divorce—that would be an unspeakable sin—but she is willing to go away for a year or two to please him; perhaps it will be better when she comes back. One evening she walks down to the bench under the cottonwood tree, as she often does when her work is finished. Then Magdalene realizes she can never leave the grave, for sitting there, she imagines the child is in her arms:

> She looked in the large eyes and felt the soft cheek against her breast. Involuntarily she clasped her arms around the imagined form and held it close. "Who will take care of the baby when

---

9. Ibid., p. 201.

you are away?" the night seemed to whisper. "Who will cut the ugly weeds which spring up on the grave late in summer? And who will stand at the kitchen window on lonely winter evenings when the cold wind howls across the prairie?"

Because Chris is gone most of the time, mother and daughter become very close, and Magdalene is determined to bring up the girl in the "ways of the fathers." Almost as strong as her mother's influence upon Mabel is the influence of the prairie. She romps outdoors to her heart's content from the time the snow disappears in the spring until it falls again in autumn, and the prairie speaks its mysterious language to her as the seasons change. To Mabel the prairie is not an obstinate force to be broken, like a wild horse, but a spirit of infinite variety, beautiful and harmonious. She does not develop her father's antagonism because she never views it solely as the storehouse of riches grudgingly yielded up.

Magdalene's mission is to bring her husband to God, and she teaches Mabel to pray for that miracle. Though Rölvaag intended Mabel to represent the fearless, devout, selfless kind of Christianity he himself admired, in these immature characterizations she and her mother do not often excite our sympathy. As Mabel grows up and becomes responsible for the care of her father, she is too often aware of the cross she carries. Her piety is frequently sanctimonious, her religious struggle superficial. She is in an almost perpetual state of uncertainty about the welfare of her soul, as though this ceaseless agitation were some insurance against damnation. It is, in fact, impossible to detect any growth in her character through the many years that pass.

During the spring floods that hit Clarkfield in 1897, Magdalene is drowned when Chris, in a blind rage, drives the buggy across a submerged bridge. In this accident he senses again nature's antagonism; it is as though the prairie were out to get him one way or another. Though he does not mourn the loss of his wife, he seethes with anger to think that after his failure to get rid of her all these years, "now long afterward when he had given it up, the prairie had taken her from him. He was absolutely certain that the prairie had tricked him, and for that trick the prairie would suffer!"

Chris descides to expand his holdings by homesteading in Canada, renting out the land in Dakota. Mabel, by now a girl of high school age, chooses to go with him out of a strong sense of duty, though he would prefer to leave her in school in the States. On New Year's Day of 1898 they leave for Alberta, where Mabel remains during the winter, while Chris goes out to survey the prairies of Saskatchewan. He shrewdly buys cheap land, believing the railroad will someday cross it and towns will spring up nearby.

In the spring he builds a cabin on a half section of land in Saskatchewan, where Mabel joins him. Conquering the prairie, he feels no need for the fellowship of men; nor does he feel any need for her, aside from her usefulness in the house and barn. He relives his experiences of twenty years earlier when he broke land in South Dakota:

> He saw land seekers roam over the prairie, a few lonely pioneers pass by; and now and then as he made the long trip to town he saw a shanty against the horizon. Not yet many houses to be seen the first two years, only immeasurable prairie, boundless as the heavens above. When he stood leaning against the plow, letting the horses take breath; when he looked back upon the fresh furrow of rich black loam, every nerve tingled with pleasure in anticipation of future wealth in what he knew would be the continent's greatest wheat bin.

Larsen attacks the prairie as though it were an enemy stubbornly withholding its riches:

> Tear it to pieces and grind it to bits. [. . .] Then we shall see what the prairie amounts to against the power of man. [. . .] He growled like a hound with jaws clamped on its prey.

Mabel is happy on the prairie; she experiences God's presence and "touche[s] His hand timidly, then thrust[s] hers safely into His." But a need for companionship turns her thoughts to her dead mother, the only friend she ever had, and she becomes morbidly concerned with her father's indifference to religion.

In the fall of 1900, a break comes in Chris Larsen's good luck. On a fine sunny day he sets out to haul his grain to market, driving two teams hitched together as he often did in Dakota.

> The vast prairie lay about him, brown and invincible in the shimmering sunlight, and overhead the sky was cool, deep blue. The untamed strength of the wild fields was still felt as the keynote of the landscape; the hand of man had not succeeded perceptibly in changing its real form.

In the farmyard, the horses are startled and break away:

> Larsen braced himself against the wagon box, twisted the lines around his hands, and pulled until the leather cut into bare flesh. [. . .] When he saw that he had not the power to stop them, rage shook his whole being; like a mighty billow it rushed through him, the insane wrath of a helpess man against an irresistible force. Between his teeth he uttered an awful curse— he would lash them to pieces when he got them stopped. He gathered all his strength for a mighty jerk but it was as though the horses had not felt it; they became even wilder. Then he did something very strange. He slackened the line, grabbed the whip, and laid it to the horses with all his might. If they wanted to go . . . they could go!

When the wheels hit a deep hole, the wagon is upset and Chris is dragged beneath it. Soon afterwards, Mabel finds him lying unconscious. From that day Chris Larsen, the child of fortune, is a cripple and never rises from his bed again.

When Chris can no longer abuse the prairie, he attacks his daughter's spirit, and Mabel is nearly broken by his ugly temper. But one night in a dream her mother speaks to her: "Now your father is returning to you; take good care of him." Believing the words mean he will eventually return to God, Mabel promises to care for her father, no matter what personal sacrifice is required. Though she is miserably discouraged at times, her conscience always brings her back to the ideal which Rölvaag called the key to the book: "When within a family one life offers itself in humility so that another can be saved, then humanity's most sacred law is fulfilled."[10]

The winter following Chris's injury is bitterly cold. One of the best chapters in the novel describes their life during the weeks when the temperature falls to forty degrees below zero. Mabel's greatest problem is the worn-out cook stove, which heats the three-room hut. The damper is broken and the fire can not be regulated:

> Either the stove would not draw or it burnt up the wood almost as fast as she put it in. It was worse when she wanted to bake bread. The loaves would stand there so beautiful and light when she had them ready for the oven that they were a delight to see, but when they had been in only a few minutes, they went flat and became only crusts of dough. [. . .] Mabel fought back the tears as bravely as she could but they came nevertheless. That winter she was often heavy-hearted because of the stove.

During much of the winter they are snowbound and Mabel cannot escape into the free spaces as she loves to do:

> Outdoors lay the solitude of the wilderness, almost palpable in the presence of the prairie buried under two feet of snow; no human being was to be seen, no dwelling or trace of man— only desolate space, eternal and immense, where the wind moaned ceaselessly, sweeping the snow around the walls of the hut, driving the cold in billows, and laying white frost in every crack.

Within the cabin her father's meanness of spirit makes life almost unendurable. Until the accident Chris has had but one aim in life, to triumph over the prairie.

> And then he had been cut so suddenly from the great purpose of his life . . . from everything else too. It had come without the slightest warning or justification. A mighty fist had pushed him out of the struggle, knocked him over, thoroughly mauled him. But the prairie—she lay out there, big and strong and rich as ever. Yea, a thousand times richer now since his hold on her had slipped.

---

10. Marginal note on the Nickerson manuscript.

Bedridden, he nurtures the churning rage he feels toward life.

The arrival of Pastor McGregor on skis one afternoon is Mabel's happiest experience since coming to Saskatchewan. An elderly man, kind and dignified, he fixes the damper in the stove so that once again she can bake respectable bread. But Pastor McGregor and Chris do not get along; Larsen speaks insultingly of the clergy and insists that self-reliant men have no need of the church. Alone with Mabel, the pastor tells her that what she is doing for her father is all God expects of her, that she is not responsible for his unregenerate condition. For the first time in many months she finds peace.

In part 2 Chris and Mabel are back in Dakota. It is impossible to care for him properly in the wilderness, and they return to their home in Clarkfield during the spring of 1901. A new fear now enters Chris's mind: that Mabel will marry and desert him. He suspects that she and Harry Haugland, the parochial school teacher, are in love. In Haugland Rölvaag shows his scorn for a type of churchman he disliked intensely: the egotistical, pompous, theatrical sort parading his way through his duties. Haugland talks about "the greatest good for the greatest number" and the importance of social service but cares little for the individual soul that is Rölvaag's chief concern. He is a second-generation Norwegian-American living in a cultural vacuum, ashamed of the language of his fathers and striving to attain the symbols of material success. In part 2 Rölvaag emphasizes the difference between Mabel's life of active service and Haugland's eternal prating about the work to be done.

In direct contrast with the fatuous Harry Haugland is the mission pastor, Skjarve, who comes to the Clarkfield church one Sunday. Like Mabel he has devoted a lifetime to serving others. The venerable old man preaches simply and directly from heartfelt convictions, the people listening eagerly to a sermon lasting an hour and a half. He describes his travels throughout the United States in behalf of home missions and expresses concern for Norwegians in America—the farmers, West Coast fishermen, Great Lakes seamen, pioneers on the Canadian prairie, and laborers in the great cities. He assumes the responsibility of helping these spiritually hungry immigrants to create a dynamic culture. Haugland seems even more ridiculous in comparison with Skjarve and, as Rölvaag admits, is an ingenuous way of voicing his own indignation at "the boys and girls who gather at young people's meetings and in Luther Leagues braying a great deal about service and the greatness of service."[11]

One detects in this novel a hint of the problem which becomes crucial in *Their Fathers' God:* the difficulties caused by marriage between members of different faiths. Rölvaag's concept of loyalty to tradition emphasizes the need for religious continuity. Among first-generation Norwegian-Americans there was almost no marriage between Lutherans and Catholics; however, in later generations intermarriage became an increasingly frequent occurrence. Rölvaag's concern is not theological; he is interested only in the difficulties that arise when cultural roots have withered sufficiently to permit such marriages. In *On Forgotten Paths* Larsen's neighbors, the Oplands, are distressed when their daughter gets in trouble "with that Irishman on the western prairie" and has to marry him. "That once did Mrs. Opland rebel against fate:—Good gracious—Irish, and then unregenerate Catholic at that!"

Finally Mabel falls in love—with Einar Haugen, the new minister, a fiery idealist, a man of action and conviction, but certainly not a wholly likable fellow. He is determined to preach the law, no matter what it costs, though there is a suggestion that his love for Mabel increases his charity. Chris learns of their affair and is able to separate them, for Mabel's conviction that her life's mission is to reclaim her father's soul demands even that she renounce Haugen.

One day when Larsen is alone in the house, a lamp below a rack of papers starts a fire, which he is helpless to put out. As the

---

11. Quoted in Jorgenson and Solum, *Rölvaag*, p. 199.

building bursts into flames, a passer-by carries out the unconscious invalid and takes him next door, where Mabel finds him. During the fire Chris cried out for God's mercy for the first time in his life. Thus, during his last days, with Mabel's help, he is brought back to "the forgotten paths" and dies a saved man, begging her forgiveness and promising to tell her mother in heaven how faithful she has been. Mabel is now free to write to Haugen and promise she will marry him.

Since its theme is the conflict between good and evil for the possession of a soul, the chief flaw in *On Forgotten Paths* is Chris Larsen's unmitigated worthlessness. There is no sense of struggle in the novel. Though Mabel may be the good angel working zealously to redeem her father, never does he show that he recognizes a difference between good and evil or that he is interested even momentarily in allying himself with good. Larsen's salvation is miraculously accomplished, and except for his fear-crazed cry for God's help as the house burns, he has no part in it. It is salvation brought about by God and an intercessor, a totally unbelievable redemption.

Though *On Forgotten Paths* is Rölvaag's least successful major work, its importance in his development is great, for it was his first attempt to write a full-scale novel in which the complications of structure, character, and plot are unified through the expression of an integral idea. But it is even more significant that in this awkward beginning appear in a germinal state basic attitudes and themes which eventually flourish, particularly in *Giants in the Earth* but also in the succeeding volumes of the trilogy.

# 4

# *THE*
# *PERIL OF ROOTLESSNESS:*
## *pure gold AND*
## *the boat of longing*

$A$side from their biographic and genetic interest, Rölvaag's first two published novels have little value; not until the appearance of his next work do we recognize a maturing talent. In 1920, Augsburg Publishing House of Minneapolis published *Two Fools: A Scene from Today (To Tullinger: Et Billede fra Idag).* Like its predecessors, it achieved only a limited circulation, mainly among Norwegian-Americans of the Middle West; and it created a furor among ultra conservative members of the Norwegian Lutheran Church of America, who considered the degeneration of Louis and Lizzie blasphemous and the satiric portrait of the pastor an attack upon the clergy.[1] Yet it did more than either of the earlier novels to bring Rölvaag the attention he deserved. A work of considerable merit, *Two Fools* exploits with a surer touch the same theme that underlies *On Forgotten Paths:* the destruction of the soul through greed.

The original version of *Two Fools* has never been translated into English; however, a revision called *Pure Gold,* prepared by Rölvaag and Sivert Erdahl, appeared in 1930. Although there were extensive stylistic changes, the plot and theme remain the same, and the attitudes are essentially those of the Norwegian text.[2]

---

1. The author's father, a Norwegian-Lutheran clergyman, recalled that many pastors never forgave Rölvaag for writing *To Tullinger,* which they scornfully referred to as *Tre Tullinger* (the third fool being Rölvaag himself). Even *Giants in the Earth* was attacked by these ultraconservatives as irreligious.

2. For a discussion of structural and stylistic changes in the revision, see Jorgenson and Solum, *Rölvaag,* pp. 402 ff.

## Rölvaag: His Life and Art

In the ten years between *Two Fools* and *Pure Gold,* Rölvaag had written his masterpiece, *Giants in the Earth,* and the second book of the trilogy, *Peder Victorious;* thus, it is to be expected that the revision shows signs of maturity lacking in *Two Fools*—deepening of tone, finer realization of character, sharper irony, and richer metaphor.[3]

Several comparisons will illustrate the differences between the two versions. In *Pure Gold* Rölvaag describes more precisely the behavior of his main characters, especially Lizzie, and emphasizes the sexual quality of her desire for possessions, as in the description of her reaction to the first gold piece she has ever seen:

> Lizzie sat there and looked at him as he explained.—Her strong features became softer as he progressed. Finer, somehow. Her large face filled with something that impressed Louis as tenderness and sweetness, almost as when she came to him the first days after the wedding and impelled him to kiss her. Finally she said with strange wonder, "You are not so stupid, Louis." [*Two Fools,* p. 28].

> At first Lizzie never answered a word. She wrapped the gold piece in her apron; the act seemed to be done unconsciously. But as he talked on she turned her face toward him; her eyes were half closed, almost hidden by the lashes; her angular features had softened to warm tenderness; in them lay an expression he had not seen there since those first nights after they were married, when she would pull the shades of the bedroom window down low before she began to undress, and he had sensed a mysterious force emanating from her that made him tremble. Now it was upon her again . . . . Gosh almighty, what a girl! [*Pure Gold,* p. 36].[4]

---

3. For the purpose of this study, the discussion is concerned mainly with the revision.

4. O. E. Rölvaag, *Pure Gold,* translated and revised by Sivert Erdahl and O. E. Rölvaag (New York: Harper and Brothers Publishers, 1930). This work is based on O. E. Rölvaag, *To Tullinger: Et Billede fra Idag* (Minneapolis: Augsburg Publishing House, 1920). Page references in the text are to these editions.

## The Peril of Rootlessness

Throughout the revision one notes an increased use of figurative language in key passages, as in this description of the quality of Louis's mind:

> Louis didn't think nearly as quickly as Lizzie. Ideas came to him slowly and stayed in his mind a long time before he did anything with them. [*Two Fools*, p. 37]
> Louis could not think as fast as Lizzie; with him ideas gerinated slowly, as the corn in a cold season; but once planted, the idea would lie there and, perhaps by and by, develop into long series of thought. [*Pure Gold*, p. 50]

In the revision Rölvaag frequently expands matter-of-fact transitional passages to heighten the tone of subsequent chapters and to evoke more fully the sweep of time:

> —Time passed. And now so swiftly that neither Louis nor Lizzie realized it. They did not have time to notice. [*Two Fools*, p. 138]
> Time passed; silent, calm-eyed, inexorable; unnoticed by most; unchallenged by all; but adding seasons and periods to every living creature, and day unto yesterday: to the young, strength and golden aspirations; to manhood, maturity and the fullness of life; casting its soft, thin mantle of hoar-frost upon those who had begun to age; no one escaped the touch of the unseen hand; but few took notice thereof. The Houglums least of all, because they could not afford to stop and look. [*Pure Gold*, p. 193]

Louis and Lizzie are more fully drawn in the revision than in the original. For example, in the early chapters, describing their courtship and honeymoon, they are portrayed as rather appealing lovers, responsive and warmhearted; thus we are more affected by their later mental and moral collapse. Compare, also, the change in Lizzie's attitude toward her husband as it is shown in the description of her reaction to Louis's terror after the farmhouse has been burned by hoodlums:

> Then she went up to him.—In that instant Lizzie could have trounced her husband. But his great fear was so entirely child-

ish in its intensity that she was touched, and so she sat down
in the hay. He begged and entreated her to lie down again
until daylight. [*Two Fools*, p. 176]

After circling about the heap of ashes, she remembered Louis,
and went back into the loft to see about him. She laughed
bitterly to herself. How scared he had been! Up in the hay
she found a groaning, stinking heap that was breathing and
had life, but was not a man, nor a human being, just an
animal wallowing in its own filth. She sat down and sobbed,
partly from anger, partly from pity. "Get yourself out of here,
you dirty old ape, and change your clothes!" she croaked.
[*Pure Gold* p. 255]

In the original advertising, *Two Fools* is called a "humorous"
book. The reader of *Pure Gold*, who sees little to laugh at in the
degeneration of Louis and Lizzie, finds such a description incon-
gruous; however, in portions of the Norwegian edition there is an
almost imperceptible gaiety missing from the English. Though
the story is equally grim in both versions, the bareness and understatement of the Norwegian allow for a wry humor lost in the more
intensely serious *Pure Gold*. The same humorous incidents occur
in both: the lighthearted courting of Louis and Lizzie and the
coarse jesting of his companions about their affair; Louis's frantic
but unsuccessful attempts to quit smoking; the reaction of the
bank tellers to the stench of the bills from Louis's money belt;
Lizzie's eagerness to believe the stranger's obviously fraudulent
story about the gold mine; and the exposure of her penchant for
lying, when she is tricked into claiming she was present at the
Biblical wedding in Cana. But in the English version these incidents seem more dismal than humorous.

Other significant changes in *Pure Gold* are the suggestions of
physical love between Lizzie and Louis in the early years of their
marriage and the addition of occasional profanity, particularly in
Louis's speeches (the Norwegian edition, approved by the publications board of the Norwegian Lutheran Church of America, carefully avoided including realistic details which might offend the
average church reader of the day). Rölvaag also reorganized the

*Photograph courtesy of the author*

Dönnes church, on Dönna Island, Norway, where Rölvaag's ancestors are buried and where he was baptized and confirmed.

Photograph courtesy of the author

Syv Söstre (Seven Sisters), mountains to the east of Dönna; "though troll maidens turned to stone, [they] still exercised their evil powers" (p. 4).

*Photograph courtesy of the author*

Dönmannen (The Man of Dönna), on the southern tip of the island—"a rock ridge shaped like a man lying dead" (p. 4).

On June 14, 1905, Rölvaag was graduated with honors from St. Olaf College.

Photograph courtesy of St. Olaf News Bureau

Rölvaag (second from left) and three of his colleagues on the faculty at St. Olaf about 1906.

Photograph courtesy of Karl F. Rolvaag

The cabin on Big Island Lake, near Marcell, Minnesota, where Rölvaag wrote most of *Giants in the Earth*. This snapshot was taken on August 17, 1923, shortly after he began intensive work on his masterpiece.

*Photograph courtesy of St. Olaf News Bureau*

Rölvaag in the garden of his home in Northfield, Minnesota. The photograph probably was taken about the time *Giants in the Earth* appeared as a Book of the Month Club selection in June, 1927.

*Photograph courtesy of St. Olaf News Bureau*

Rölvaag at St. Olaf College in 1929, autographing copies of *Peder Victorious*, the second novel of his trilogy of pioneer life.

original twenty-nine chapters into five major sections, each with its own title and theme. But in spite of the changes, most of which were an improvement, the revision is not greatly superior to the original, for Rölvaag was unable to intensify the impression of futility in the lives of his protagonists.

When the title *Pure Gold* was substituted for *Two Fools,* Rölvaag added a scriptural epigraph to suggest the theme implicit in the Norwegian title: "But God said unto him, 'Thou fool, this night thy soul shall be required of thee; then whose shall those things be, which thou hast provided?'" The theme is the ancient one of the fate of those who barter their souls for riches, but it is the essence of Rölvaag's rendering that Louis and Lizzie are second-generation Norwegian-Americans whose rootlessness shapes their attitudes. Lizzie ridicules tradition and scornfully abjures all ties with the past. Eventually the force of her will overpowers Louis's gentle nature, suppressing any expression of spiritual need, which she considers a sign of weakness. Though Rölvaag relates their story to a specific cultural environment, by extension he is illustrating the peril of rootlessness to all immigrants.

The story covers a span of twenty years, beginning shortly after 1900, and takes place in Greenfield, Minnesota, which is also the setting of an earlier fragment about a pioneer pastor and of Rölvaag's first attempt at a novel, *Nils and Astri.* Louis and Lizzie are the only major characters, although as the story unfolds their money almost becomes a character too.

Lizzie first appears as a high-spirited girl, "well past twenty-five," who is cooking for the threshers on her father's farm. Her interest fastens upon Lars Houglum, whose strength and muscular body attract her, and she stands watching at the door as he pounds stakes to hold the threshing machine. It is a warm autumn afternoon with a clear blue sky, the mood deceptively suggestive of a Minnesota pastoral.

Lars, one of the owners of the machine, also has two teams of horses, and people say about him "that he took better care of his horses than he did of himself" (p. 5). In Lars's pride of possession we have the only hint of the selfishness which grows into over-mastering avarice. Lars is drawn to Lizzie, sensing her interest in him and admiring her tenacity and determination. The two remind us of Trina and the title character in *McTeague,* Frank Norris's 1899 study of greed. Like McTeague, Lars is slow-witted though instinctively kind and gentle:

> He was saving and sober, a steady worker; no fooling of any kind. The prairie needed just such men . . . such always made headway . . . . Yet Lars didn't seem to be getting there very fast . . . . [Lizzie's father] turned the problem in his mind . . . . The share in the threshing rig must be all he owned? And threshing was a poor business in the long run . . . . The other thing he had heard said about Lars, that he was slow with books and such matters, would not make so much difference. One could get along all right without knowing much about books—Tom knew that. [P. 14]

Lizzie, like Trina, is shrewd and practical, revealing from the beginning a voracious selfishness. After proposing to Lars, who lacks courage enough to ask her to marry him, she determines that he must give up the itinerant life of a thresher and settle down on their own farm, where they can live more prosperously. The money for a down payment will come from the sale of the rig and a loan from her father, who owes her at least that much for her years of service.

Throughout their engagement Lizzie plans for the day when they will begin to get ahead although she has little faith in her husband's dependability:

> If only Lars could manage his end of it! Not that she didn't intend to help him with the outside work, too. But Lars wasn't very strong on planning and such like—no one is perfect in everything, anyway. [P. 20]

But she desires him possessively and dreams of their farm "as a world they ruled over . . . only the two of them in their own universe!" (p. 20).

One thing disturbs her in these plans for the future—Lars's name. She can tolerate his blundering and slowness but not that Norwegian name:

> Lars sounded so foreign; it wasn't a bit nice, either; she'd call him *Louis;* that was American. Now listen to this: Mrs. Louis Houglum—Mrs. Lizzie M. Houglum, oh, there was a name to feel proud of! And other things, too, she'd do with him; Lars was so strong and helpless, just like a little boy who hadn't had any care for a long time. [P. 22]

Lars is not pleased with Lizzie's plan to change his name but reluctantly submits to being called "Louis." He flatly refuses, however, to call her "Maggie" as she wishes. Her baptismal name is also a distinctly Norwegian one—Lisbet Marie. But long ago at school she read a novel in which the heroine was named Maggie. Since then she has loved the name and wished it her own. Her teacher encouraged her to call herself "Maggie":

> America was a free country, and this custom of having ignorant parents fasten upon an innocent child a name which she detested was nothing but a remnant of barbarism. What right did a parent have thus to embitter a child's life? Lizzy was very happy that night but at home she met with an indignant rebuff. [. . .] And now the suggestion did not meet with Lars's favour, either. [P. 23]

Thus Rölvaag expresses one aspect of Lizzie's antagonism toward her heritage.

After their marriage Lizzie's increasing avarice infects Louis. Each of them does the work of two people, living only to pay off the mortgage and own the farm outright. When Louis is in town selling corn, Lizzie is uneasy for fear "sharpers" will take advantage of him. She milks the three cows to the last drop, wishing they had at least one more animal, and resolves to ask her father for another. In order to save a few dollars she cancels the subscription to *Skandinaven,* a Norwegian-American newspaper which Louis thoroughly enjoys. He reveals a stronger loyalty to the past than

Lizzie's when he remarks wistfully, "Father took that paper as long as he lived."

Her ruthless economizing would cut out Louis's tobacco if he would allow it, but on that point he stands his ground. When the subject comes up one day after he returns from town, he distracts her by showing her a ten-dollar gold piece, the first she has ever seen: " 'See, Lizzie, this is pure gold!' His voice had dropped low, in his eyes was a fascinated look" (p. 35). Clearly Louis's appetite has been whetted by the gold, and henceforth their lives are blighted by this new passion. So deeply is Lizzie stirred that her desire is expressed in sexual terms. That night she lies sleepless, the moon like a huge glowing gold piece framed in the window. The coin is hidden in the dresser drawer among the folds of her best handkerchief, and she frequently slips into the bedroom to admire it, though never when Louis is at home. Her chief concern is how to get her hands on more gold, and she accompanies Louis when he goes to town to settle up to make certain that he drives the shrewdest possible bargain.

Louis detects a change in her and immediately suspects pregnancy. The thought dismays him for that would mean an end to her help in the field and a decrease in their profits. But no child is ever born of their marriage. Rölvaag suggests that Lizzie's vague maternal yearning is transferred to the gold coin she hoards:

> Yes, there he lay, the sleepy-head . . . so alone and abandoned, with nobody to look after him . . . poor little dear! . . . Such a smart fellow, too. When she held him up to the light he seemed to waken, smile, and beam at her; there was a twinkle for every turn. [P. 42]

Inevitably she comes to look upon the increasing store of coins as her "babies."

Early in their marriage Lizzie jokingly referred to herself as Louis's "hired hand"; now she begins to take her role seriously and demands wages in order to put money away systematically. Only five years after buying the farm, they pay off the mortgage.

## The Peril of Rootlessness

Whatever they make is clear profit, and they work with a vengeance. People in the community say they have picked the old folks clean, and it is common knowledge that they refuse to contribute to the support of their pastor.

Soon they have two thousand dollars hidden in various places in the house—some in bills, some in silver, and some in ten-dollar gold pieces—and use a code to refer to their money: the gold pieces are "babies," the bank notes "brats," and the silver dollars "shillings." Learning that the house of a neighbor has been destroyed by fire and with it six hundred dollars in paper money, Lizzie and Louis are terrified lest such an accident befall them. Shortly afterwards, they put eight hundred dollars of their money in the bank, Louis keeping most of the rest of it on his person, even when he goes to bed at night. Two years later the bank fails, and for Lizzie and Louis it seems like the end of the world.

The bank crash is the turning point in their lives. Louis shares Lizzie's resentment of fate for robbing them, but the blow is harder for Lizzie to bear, since she had "mothered" all those precious dollars:

> And she had tended them so well, making them comfortable, had watched over each one with such anxious care: they were hers—part of her own self . . . now they were gone irrevocably, never to return. She had been lured into ambush and wantonly stripped! [Pp. 109–10]

From now on they are suspicious of everyone and everything, always on guard lest they be cheated by their fellow men. Determined to make up their loss, they live even more frugally, patching old clothing and shoes and skimping on food.

Their suspicion of others does not prevent Lizzie's being swindled by a stranger who comes to the house asking for food. She is ready to turn him away, but something about him fascinates her—he is dressed in black—and besides, he offers to pay for his meal. He speaks only Norwegian to Lizzie, and she would be certain he is a minister except that nowadays ministers no longer take the trouble to speak Norwegian to people who readily understand English. He agrees to pay her liberally for a room to use as head-quarters while tending to important business in the area.

That evening Lizzie, insatiably curious about his activities, draws from him the admission that he is selling mining stock which is expected to return $150,000 for each $1,000 invested. The stranger shows them the gold he carries in his money belt—gold which they will share if they invest in the mine. As in Rölvaag's next novel, *The Boat of Longing*, the stranger dressed in black, with his promise of wordly gain not to be found in the paths of the fathers, suggests the devil. He symbolizes the materialism which competes with native cultural values, the immigrants' true wealth in America. Lizzie's avarice is so great that she decides to invest $1,000, though Louis suspects fraud. After a terrible argument she demands that they divide their money so each can do with his what he chooses. Louis, still devoted to her, is ashamed of the implications of such an act, but Lizzie despises him for fearing to take a chance that might bring them a fortune.

From the moment they first consider dividing the money, a breach between them is inevitable. Lizzie withdraws into dreams of the gold her investment will bring and even plans how she will spend some of it. A year passes while she fretfully counts the days "as one whose time of birthing is drawing near." Finally a letter comes, telling of the failure of the mining venture. The shock is so great that she never entirely recovers from it. The rift between husband and wife widens and Louis begins to hoard secretly, intending at first only to get back his half of the thousand dollars which Lizzie lost. He makes new money belts for both of them, like the one in which the stranger carried samples of gold, and they never remove them from their bodies.

The coming of World War I brings rising farm prices, and they soon carry eight thousand dollars each in bills. But disaster visits them again, this time in the form of the liberty loan and charity drives to which they are repeatedly urged to subscribe. Because of their refusal the community turns against them, and their isolation is more complete than ever before. In Hazel Knapp, chairman of the Red Cross Auxiliary, Rölvaag has drawn a satiric—and hopelessly unconvincing—portrait of another rootless second-generation Norwegian-American who has renounced her heritage.

> Take her name, for example—Hazel Knapp, so short and with such a snap to it, with no trace of foreign origin, neither in sound nor in spelling. The old folks still persisted in using the old form Knapperud, which was a source of constant annoyance to Hazel; but she just couldn't make them drop it. Old folks are so stupid! The other young Knapperuds—there were thirteen, all told—agreed with her perfectly; it was an ugly duckling of a name, and more: absolutely impossible in this country! Good heavens! What chance would a young American have going around with a pump-handle of a name like that? No chance at all. Real Americans would think that they had come over from Norway only yesterday, and would call them greenhorns and dirty foreigners. [P. 229]

Rölvaag's own indignation at the American attitude toward foreigners, which took many ugly forms during the war years, is obvious in his characterization of Hazel Knapp, and mars it.

When the Houglums refuse to respond to the war time appeals, Hazel complains that someone ought "to teach such people a lesson." One Saturday night a group of town loiterers drive out to the farm, hoping to give Louis and Lizzie the scare of their lives. They build a large bonfire and set up a flagpole nearby, intending to force the Houglums to kneel at its foot and take an oath of allegiance. But the boys have been drinking and their plans go awry. Louis and Lizzie, suspecting trouble, are hidden in the barn, and in the search for them the house is accidentally set afire. Rölvaag uses the flaming building to suggest the hysteria of the war years which has taken hold of even this normally peaceful community.

Rather than build anew Lizzie and Louis remodel the chicken house and move into it. But their days on the farm are soon over. In the excitement caused by rising land prices, most farms in the neighborhood have been sold, some two and three times. Men thoughtlessly cut themselves off from the familiar soil into which they have sunk roots:

> It happened repeatedly that the man who had carved a home out of the wilderness got up and left his homestead as though it were a wornout garment he had sold to the highest bidder. Nothing was any longer held sacred. [P. 262]

When the Houglums are offered $250 an acre for their farm, they cannot refuse it. Only Louis feels any immediate regret at leaving:

> As they drove down the yard his eyes watered so that he could not see. The whole farm lay quiet and deserted. No life to be seen anywhere. Not a sound; not even a rooster crowed. The henhouse looked so squatty and forlorn . . . . Well, good-bye, old farm. [Pp. 271–72]

In town they rent two shabby rooms above a store for seven dollars a month, though each carries thirty-five thousand dollars in his money belt. Lizzie works as a maid and dishwasher because she cannot bear to part with even a penny of her hoard, and Louis at her urging takes a job as section hand on the railroad. One day early in November Louis overhears two men discussing an event of great importance soon to occur. Curious, he joins the conversation and is shown an article in a Norwegian-American newspaper prophesying the approaching end of the world. The sober talk of the fanatics disturbs him, and he goes to the new minister for advice and comfort. The pastor, of Norwegian ancestry, rejects the Norwegian language and endeavors to wipe out any trace of "foreignism" in the community. He tells Louis that he does not read *Skandinaven:* "I don't believe in taking a Norwegian newspaper, and thus helping to perpetuate a foreign language press in America" (p. 301). The pastor then questions him about his church membership and contributions in such an unfriendly manner that Louis is unable to broach the subject he came to discuss. He leaves, more dispirited than ever, and goes home to ponder the prophecy of the fanatics.

Through the years he has kept out from their savings a thousand dollars which rightfully belongs to Lizzie. Tormented by the fear that he will die while it is still in his possession, Louis tries and fails to restore the money to her without her knowledge. As a last resort, he shows her the article in *Skandinaven*, hoping to win her sympathy so that he can confess his theft. Instead Lizzie flies into a rage and berates him for his cowardice. To escape her wrath, he goes to church alone that Sunday morning and hears a sermon on the three paths leading to destruction: drunkenness, adultery, and greed for gold. When the service is over Louis, desperate for comfort, walks out into the country to see his two horses again, hoping to find in them some trace of affection:

> Louis went into Jim's stall first, petting the horse all over. But he couldn't stay there long. When Fan's turn came he slipped his arm about her neck, uttering low cries, half human and half that of a mother beast that has lost her young and then, unexpectedly, has found them. A dam somewhere within him had burst open, and now he couldn't stop the rushing flood. With his cheek pressed against Fanny's skinny neck he sobbed convulsively. [P. 320]

On the way home Louis loses his way in the snow and stumbles upon the house of the man who first told him about the approaching end of the world. Hungry and exhausted, he rests while the fanatic prays for his salvation, then sets out to walk the twelve miles back to town and again loses his way.

> Big tears ran down his face and into his open mouth. He dragged his feet after him, like a child that has grown tired and is giving up. A queer, unreasonable desire came over him: to fall on his knees and talk to someone . . . . No, no! He must go on, and get home as soon as possible! . . . He must pay back that thousand dollars. [P. 332]

In town Lizzie waits in the dark unheated apartment, certain that a tramp has waylaid Louis and taken his money. Gradually the numbing cold overpowers her. Hearing someone crawling up the stairs, she imagines a thief coming to rob her. With an ax by her side, she clings to the door knob, listening to the rasping noises in the corridor:

> The knob gave a twist and a hard jerk. Lizzie heard deep moanings come out of a dark cavern . . . felt another twist and more frantic jerkings. For the space of many hours, so it seemed to her, all was still as in a grave . . . the huge bulk, that must weigh tons, sank in a heap right up against the door . . . there was another unearthly groan, and all was stiller than death itself. [P. 341]

Then Lizzie's strength gives way and she collapses beside the door. Three days later their frozen bodies are discovered. The doctor orders everything they are wearing burned because of the danger of influenza. The undertaker cuts off the money belts and throws them in with the clothes and, in the evening after all the people have left the store below the apartment, makes a bonfire behind the building, the smoke curling into the frosty air:

> The paper which had been wrapped around the clothes and the clothes themselves gave a cheerful flame. The belts went more slowly. But gradually they too changed into slender columns of blue smoke which mingled with the calm, deep night and was gone. [P. 346]

Louis and Lizzie are defeated because they do not love the land. Like Chris Larsen, the power-mad pioneer in *On Forgotten Paths,* they crave the riches the prairie offers and abandon their heritage in order to possess them. Though the prairie treats them generously, they demand ever more. In the ensuing struggle "the great brooding troll" exacts its vengeance: the souls of these two who seek dominion in the kingdom of this world. No miraculous intervention redeems Louis and Lizzie, no sudden act of faith, as in *On Forgotten Paths,* saves them from the destruction toward which they are heading. Rölvaag presents convincingly the disintegration of two rootless beings whose isolation is the cause of their sterile lives. What their souls are worth is suggested by the thin column of blue smoke ascending into the night.

# The Peril of Rootlessness

*Pure Gold* is more than "an old-fashioned story of the melodramatic miser with a fat role for character actors who are fond of rubbing their palms to denote greed, listening for the clink of gold and cackling half madly in the throes of their covetous emotions."[5] It is a novel of moral force and unerring psychological delineation in which the protagonists are not victimized by life but are their own destroyers. Nowhere has Rölvaag shown more vividly than in *Pure Gold* the danger to men in isolating themselves from humankind.

In his next novel, *The Boat of Longing* (1921), Rölvaag's attention is still focused on the problem of successful immigrant transplantation in America. But instead of depicting the defeat of his central characters in a materialistic society as in *Pure Gold,* he tells of a would-be artist who remains true to the vision of his peculiar mission in the face of almost insurmountable difficulties. Like *Letters from America, The Boat of Longing* concerns a young Norwegian who immigrates to the Middle West, but where Per of the *Letters* is basically an optimistic, enterprising, sociable being to whom life in the New World is an adventure eagerly enjoyed, Nils is a hypersensitive, introspective young man upon whose finely wrought artistic nature the spiritual climate of America has a corrosive effect. Both of these characters, of course, represent aspects of Rölvaag's own personality, though it is with Nils that one most readily compares him.[6]

In *The Boat of Longing* Rölvaag develops three central themes: the initial commitment of the protagonist to a life of art (in part 1); the struggle of the immigrant to retain his identity in a hostile culture (in parts 2 and 3); and the cost of immigration to those who remain behind in the Old World and suffer the loss of loved ones (in part 4).

---

5. William Soskin, review of *Pure Gold, New York Evening Post,* February 7, 1930.

6. When the author asked Mrs. Rölvaag if her husband had a favorite among his novels, she answered: "Oh, yes, *The Boat of Longing.* He always felt that it was his own story." Interview in August of 1956.

Rölvaag has been criticized for presenting a distorted view of immigrant life in America by exaggerating the difficulties facing the newcomer in making a successful adjustment. Theodore Blegen, for example, after a study of "America letters," concludes that the great majority of emigrants probably were content with their choice.[7] In his view emigration was perhaps not so tragic as it often seemed. The break with the homeland represented not so much a complete rupture as a transition to a new way of life, primarily through an adjustment in language; for as the old language atrophied, the new one became enriched.[8] Yet Rölvaag insisted that this novel is not to be considered a picture of immigrant life generally in the larger cities of the Middle West but of only one sensitive soul "making an effort to adjust itself in a new land and in a pioneering country."[9] His purpose as expressed in the novel's epigraph is to rescue the individual personality from the crushing anonymity of life in America, to invalidate the "belief that the immigrant has no soul."

It is customary to refer to *The Boat of Longing* as a tragedy in which Nils is destroyed by hostile forces. Lincoln Colcord calls it "the study of a sensitive, artistic youth who comes to America from Norway full of dreams and ideals, expecting to find all that his soul longs for; he does not find it, with the result that his life goes down in disaster."[10] Another critic asserts that the immigrant artist is inevitably destroyed by America: "Given the fact of immigration, what hope was there that the immigrant would not lose his soul. . . ? We look in vain for an encouraging answer. When the sensitive person of artistic bent emigrates, he forfeits the possibility of full self-realization."[11]

---

7. Blegen, *Norwegian Migration to America: 1825–1860*, p. 315.

8. Theodore C. Blegen, *Grass Roots History* (Minneapolis: University of Minnesota Press, 1947), p. 113.

9. Quoted in Jorgenson and Solum, *Ole Edvart Rölvaag*, p. 284.

10. Colcord, Introduction to *Giants in the Earth* (1927 ed.), p. xxx.

11. See Stevens, "Rölvaag," p. 70.

## The Peril of Rootlessness

Rölvaag could not have believed that Nils's life "goes down in disaster," although he himself referred to the tragedy of Nils's struggle to maintain his identity in America. His own literary achievement, as he frequently observed, depended on experience in two worlds. Not all immigrants lose their souls in America— only those who remain adrift. We are given reason to hope that Nils will be true to the vision of his special potentialities. It is implicit in his acceptance of Kristine Dahl's violin, which is to go only to "good hands . . . that won't shame it." Moreover, he is made of better stuff than the alcoholic poet Weismann, who recognizes in him the potentialities of the *askeladd* of his beloved fairy tales. Nils's concern is to know men, to observe them in order to understand life better. Accepting the violin symbolizes his consecration to goals which distinguish him from his companions.

Rölvaag's pessimism in this novel grows out of his belief that the materialism of America frustrates rather than encourages spiritual growth. The real tragedy, as one reviewer has observed, is neither "the personal one of the stricken old people back home, nor the seeming impossibility of the immigrant boy to find himself in his new environment. It lies in the fact that two cultures meet in a contact wherein the worst of each is exposed to the other."[12]

The central symbol of *The Boat of Longing* is a mysterious craft which appears in the Norwegian Sea, bathed in the shimmer of the midnight sun, then vanishes instantly. Its appearance, always in a moment of crisis, signifies fulfillment, sometimes through happiness and sometimes through grief. Whoever sees the shining boat will experience a profound change. George W. Spohn observes that although the boat's "uncanny drawing power induces many to start in pursuit of it . . . no report of its essential nature is ever brought back. After all it is the symbol of something that lies too deep within the heart to be reduced to a tangible phenomenon."[13]

---

12. Fred T. Marsh, "Rölvaag's Fifth and Last Novel," *New York Herald-Tribune,* January 22, 1933.

13. George W. Spohn, review of *The Boat of Longing, Manitou Messenger* (St. Olaf College newspaper), January 17, 1933.

## Rölvaag: His Life and Art

As a child Rölvaag undoubtedly heard tales of a mysterious boat which figures prominently in Norwegian folklore. He perhaps knew such a story as "The Three Princesses of Whiteland," which tells of a magic craft that carries a fisherlad to the far-off wonderful world of Whiteland.[14] It is unlikely, however, than any particular source provided him with a legend so familiar to the seafaring people among whom he lived.

The first of the four parts of *The Boat of Longing*, "The Cove Under the Hill," ranks with Rölvaag's best writing. It is thoroughly Norwegian in mood and tone, the language even in translation retaining the peculiar flavor of his native dialect. One notes a distinctly Germanic quality in his frequent use of understatement and gnomic sayings, and throughout the entire section one feels the rhythm of the sea. Supernatural powers reveal themselves in omens as well as in the actions of strange characters like the enchantress Finne-Katrine and the pastor, with his other-worldly knowledge.

Certain influences of Jonas Lie's *The Visionary* (1870) upon this part of the novel may be noted. Lie's visionary has the poetic insight characteristic of Rölvaag's Nils, who is also a kind of visionary; and in both novels the vision equates with truth. In both we note the presence of a dark-skinned foreigner with passionate eyes, who brings gaiety and laughter into the solemn lives of the Norwegians. Furthermore, David, like Nils, expresses his longing through playing the violin. Though he sometimes plays classical compositions to bring balance to his mind, David prefers to indulge in fantasy—like Nils, who surrenders to "the Boat of Longing." These two Nordlændings are both out of place in a civilization where in order to get ahead they must exploit intelligence at the expense of imagination. In both novels the heroes achieve manhood through disappointment in love. Finally, Rölvaag's Finne-Katrine, mysterious and pagan, is much like Lie's Anna Kvæn.

---

14. George Webbe Dasent, ed., *A Collection of Popular Tales from the Norse and North German*, vol. 13 of *Anglo-Saxon Classics*, ed. Rasmus B. Anderson (London: The Norrœna Society, 1905), pp. 203–10.

# The Peril of Rootlessness

After an account of various appearances of the mysterious boat westward in the open sea, a vision accompanied at times by ethereal music, Rölvaag introduces a new symbol in Zalma, the "dark girl," who represents the life of creative imagination. The only survivor of a shipwreck on a tiny rock island far from the mainland, she is found unconscious in a fishermen's station. The girl recovers slowly and behaves like a wild creature, fearful of her benefactors as she crouches lonely on a rock above the sea, "like a great black bird with its wings folded" (p. 13).[15] When winter comes on and the men must leave the island, she is taken by force, netted like a bird; for she "hopped from stone to stone like a sandpiper" (p. 15). While the authorities are attempting to discover her identity, the girl is tended by a fisherman, Jo by the Sea, and his wife Anna. Thanks to their good care and affection she recovers her health, but because she cannot speak their language, she remains suspicious of them and keeps apart as much as possible.

The family of Jo by the Sea is modeled upon Rölvaag's own. Jo, one of the fishermen who found the girl at the station, reveals an instinctive generosity in his offer to take her into his home. Once before he had befriended a stranger, a pauper fiddler, but the consequence of that kindness had not pleased him: the old man had taught their son, Nils, how to play the violin. In Jo there is a deep-rooted suspicion of music. He mistrusts an instrument that can bring confusion to the emotions and agitate the spirit so powerfully. By nature Jo is dark and gloomy, fearful of his feelings and of expressing them. Anna feels a greater joy in life than her husband, though she too is extremely serious by nature. Her kindliness permeates the household and mitigates the severity of Jo's control.

Their only child, Nils, born to them in their middle age, is now a boy of sixteen only recently confirmed. Shy and alone much of

---

15. Page references in the text are to O. E. Rölvaag, *The Boat of Longing*, trans. Nora Solum (New York: Harper and Brothers Publishers, 1933). Originally published as *Længselens Baat* (Minneapolis: Augsburg Publishing House, 1921).

the time, he is content to be with his parents, or in a boat on the bay, and he gives promise of becoming a first-rate seaman. Two influences dominate Nils's imagination: the sea and music. Like the boy Rölvaag, he yearns to express the thoughts and feelings which stir in him and tries to compose melodies that people will someday sing. With the "dark girl" he shares dreams of faraway things, and music finally brings them together. One evening as Nils plays for the family, her face wears a rapt expression:

> She stood harking to the tones; yet not to them either, exactly, her look more like that of one straining to catch faint, far-off sounds, uncertain just what they are. The music ceasing, she laughed, an altogether natural laugh, the first one since she had come into the house. Then she clapped her hands, her eyes taking in the room with the delight of one just entering it. After that evening, it was easier for them to make her understand their behests; and she showed more intelligence in her work. [P. 19]

The song that she loves most, the one that brings them together, is of his own making, the melody always the same but played sometimes as laughter, sometimes as tears, its harmony inspired by the wondrous and beautiful sea. When Nils has finished playing, the girl sings in her own language and dances to express her moods. Like Nils's song, hers begins in deep sorrow but ends in sheer joy. Finally, she throws her arms around him and hugs him laughingly.

On one level, this scene conveys the realization of Nils and the girl that they are in love; on a deeper level, it represents Nils's consecration as an artist. When he embraces the "dark girl" and aligns his spirit with hers, he accepts the imaginative world she signifies: beauty, mystery, sorrow, elemental passion. The father, observing their joy, is filled with dissatisfaction. From that moment, happiness departs from his life. Unwilling to enter the world of the imagination, his stubbornly logical mind sees in Nils's behavior subjection to a destructive influence. Though Anna afterwards accepts the girl fully, the father continues to view her with suspicion. His response reflects the rigidly pietistic attitude toward the

## The Peril of Rootlessness

arts which holds that if they are not actually inspired by the devil, they are at best a great waste of time and effort.

One day the girl suddenly remembers her name, Zalma, and laughs at Nils because he cannot pronounce it correctly. Observing that his son is upset by her laughter and fearing her power over him, Jo resolves that she must leave. He is angered by Anna's defense of Zalma and especially by her suggestion that perhaps Nils and the girl belong together:

> Could she, the mother, be wishing their only child so much ill? Was she really so indifferent about the boy's future that she could see no further than that? Couldn't she see that all was not right with this person? Wasn't she going here practising her tricks on him, trying to bewitch him—if she hadn't already succeeded? Didn't the gleam in her eyes tell her that she was a sorceress? [P. 25]

Now not even Anna's gentle nature can restore harmony in the cottage or dispel the gloom that settles over their lives.

Jo succeeds finally in having the girl removed. She has been identified as the daughter of a Jewish goldsmith and will be sent back to her family in Russia. One day while Jo and Nils are fishing, the authorities come for her. It is difficult for Anna to give her up, and Zalma herself is reluctant to go; yet thoughts of home fill her mind, and she laughs when she understands what is to happen. But she does not want to leave without saying goodbye to Nils. Throwing her arms about Anna, she weeps violently.

That night when the men return, Nils discovers that Zalma is gone. Soon afterwards all three of them, as they stand on the shore looking westward, see the Boat of Longing. It is Nils who glimpses it first. As he points it out to the others, a chill sweeps over them. There it lies, sails golden in the midnight sun. An irresistible impulse takes hold of him; he jumps into the skiff and rows furiously toward the mysterious boat in the open sea until he disappears from view.

To Nils the boat brings back Zalma's song and his own yearning to express the music within him. In the sunny night, as he gazes

at the shining sails which never seem closer no matter how hard
he rows, he hears distant music:

> Nils gazed and gazed. And listened; strained till the blood
> whirred through his head. He was positive he heard tones
> coming from out there . . . . There! . . . No? . . . Aye, there
> they were again! . . . Not song. Nor yet the tone of an instru-
> ment. An interweaving rather of song and violin . . . . It came
> out of the sunglow. And from the sea . . . . It was there, and
> it was not there.
> "That tone," cried Nils, "I must have!" [P. 40]

In this one uniting and mystical experience are expressed his recognition of the sea as the central fact of his existence; his affinity with
the world of the imagination, represented by Zalma; and his determination to become an artist.

When Nils suddenly discovers that he is in the midst of a school
of black cod, his fisherman's practicality asserts itself and he throws
out his lines, hauling in fish until the boat is filled. This episode
has been interpreted to mean that possibly in America Nils is side-
tracked from his pursuit of a worthy life and falls prey to materialism.[16] It seems more likely that it is meant to indicate Nils's practical dedication to art, his belief that it must be ethical rather than
purely esthetic. For Rölvaag writes: ". . . in the midst of the wild
joy of battle the consciousness of his goal stood clearly before him:
he was heading straight for the Boat!" (p. 41).

After Zalma's leaving, Nils becomes increasingly dissatisfied with
life at home. Finally, when he is almost seventeen, he decides to
join the Lofoten fishing fleet, though both his father and mother
try to discourage him. He bitterly resents their attitude:

> Didn't they understand how he felt, or know what he was
> struggling with? Did they really wish him to stifle within these
> narrow limits of home, when his whole soul was crying out
> for escape . . . not to mention all those strangely disturbing
> forces which so gripped and bewildered him?

---

16. Stevens, "Rölvaag," p. 61.

. . . Well, it couldn't be helped; now that he saw the way out, he meant to take it! [P. 46]

It is impossible for the kindly mother long to remain at odds with the boy. One night when she cannot sleep, she goes to his room and finds him awake. As she holds him to her, an awareness of her great love comes over him, and he weeps like a child. Soon afterwards Nils joins the Lofoten fleet with his mother's blessing.

On the fishing expedition Nils's constant companion is Per Hansen, whose brother Otto had emigrated to America a few months earlier. In his letters Otto tells of incredible achievements and opportunities in the New World, emphasizing the wealth and ease, as well as the high social status, which even a Norwegian immigrant can enjoy.[17] He urges Per to come to Minneapolis at the first opportunity, pointing out that "this fall he had earned more in two weeks than Per would be earning this whole trip [to the Lofoten Islands]. And then there was pay day every single week. As soon as Saturday afternoon was over, you had your money in your pocket" (p. 50).

Per plans to leave for America as soon as the expedition is over and begs Nils to accompany him. The argument he uses which appeals most powerfully to Nils is that in America one can easily become what he wants to be: "Depend on it . . . if you ever get [there] you'll make a name for yourself. All you've got to do is to go around and give concerts and you'll be a millionaire right off!" (p. 55).

Nils's decision to emigrate with Per is made the afternoon he climbs Væröy Mountain in the Lofoten chain. The young Rölvaag himself had often sat upon the ridge behind the cottage at Dönna,

---

17. See Theodore C. Blegen, ed., *Land of Their Choice: The Immigrants Write Home* (Minneapolis: University of Minnesota Press, 1955). Blegen reprints in full or in excerpt several hundred letters from Norwegian immigrants. Not all reports of life in America are favorable, by any means, and some warn Norwegians not to be deceived by glowing tales and advise them to stay home. In general, however, the letters maintain that a hard-working, determined immigrant can build a far better life for himself in America than would be possible in Norway.

gazing westward toward the sea, pondering the opportunities awaiting him in America. On the mountain top Nils rededicates himself
to the creative life:

> ...As he sat there on the rock, a terrible longing gripped
> him, a longing to get out to the great and the sublime, to the
> imperishably beautiful.
> ...And he cried. Aye, he sat there crying, not knowing that
> he did it.
> ...And he prayed to the Being who had created all things
> and had made the world wondrously big and beautiful—
> prayed that He would let him go out to the great and the sub-
> lime, so that he might live it. [P. 59]

Nils knows that his father will argue against his going but that
his mother will understand.

Anna and Jo rejoice when Nils comes home from the Lofoten
expedition. Subsequently, when they go on fishing trips together,
Jo, recognizing Nils's superior seamanship, gives up his position
at the tiller. But even after repeated urging Nils never goes to pick
up his chest, which has been standing on the quay at Vik since his
return. One day when he and his mother are together in the boat,
hauling in lines, she asks:

> "Are you thinking of leaving us, Nils?"
> "Of leaving you?"
> "Aye. Are you going away from us?"
> "No. Not away from you, exactly."
> "But are you going away?"
> "Well, for a while I am."
> "Do you intend to hire out?"
> "No, that I'll not do."
> Mother Anna gave a sigh of relief. Such not being his inten-
> tion, it couldn't be so bad after all.
> "Is it a seining trip, perhaps?" she came back, lighter voiced.
> "No, it's not that either." A brief inner struggle. Then baldly:
> "I'm going to America."
> "Where, my boy?" Mother Anna held the oars; the blur made
> it almost impossible for her to distinguish him, though he sat
> directly opposite her, aft in the boat.

## The Peril of Rootlessness

"I've decided to go to America," said Nils, quietly. His face was blood red.

Neither could muster a word. A barrier of leaden inertness filled the space between them. [Pp. 68–69]

This scene illustrates Rölvaag's ability to create tension, to cut through externals and reveal the human spirit in a moment of great stress. As in Björnson's novels, the economy of language is but one step removed from pantomime. There are no words to express the misery these two endure.

When Anna gains control of her emotions, she speaks to Nils reasonably, as his father would do. She reminds him of their happy life together, of the blessings they share. Nils replies that it is good— but only a part of life and not enough. She asks for no more reasons, understanding that though she is satisfied to live beside the cove under the hill, her son is troubled by longings that cannot be fulfilled there. When she questions what he is going to become, he answers: "Oh—that which is highest of all." Her heart swells at these words, for she believes they will come true and tries not to think of the sorrow ahead. In the village that same afternoon, Jo hears by chance of his son's plans. The news plunges him into despair because he is unable to project himself into his son's dreams as Anna can. But there is no reproach, for he too loves Nils and gives him his blessing since his mind is made up.

Nils leaves in a storm, his parents accompanying him part way to the village, the three of them trudging speechless through rain and wind. Their leavetaking is the finest scene in the novel, perhaps the finest scene Rölvaag ever created. He suggests an anguish as desolate as the storm howling about them:

"You mustn't come any farther," [Nils] said.
"No," replied Jo.
"No," echoed Mother Anna, hollowly, "we'll not go any farther now,"
Nils stretched forth his hand—to the father first.
"Thanks for—!" But that was all he could muster. From the strong face before him two gleaming eyes peered at him through the rain. So stolid and shut was the look of the face in

that instant that to say what thoughts worked behind it would have baffled the most expert reader of minds.

The father took the hand, locked it hard for a moment, then dropped it; not a sound escaped his lips.

Nils offered his hand to his mother. She grasped it, clung desperately to it, could not let it go. The hand not being enough, she seized his arm, caught him close, and began to cry so convulsively that she sank upon his shoulder.

"Oh—my boy, my boy! . . . My blessed boy! . . . God reward you for the comfort you've been! . . . And God be—!"

Nils held her until her crying, having stilled itself, came more easily, like a child's.

Then with a wrench he tore himself loose and went.

Having got a little way off, he had to look back. This he had not wanted to do, but he couldn't help it.

And there through the shrieking storm and driving rain he saw the figure of his mother, plain as could be against the murky sky; but not his father's. The mother was holding her right hand high. . . . He walked on, only to turn again. The figure had not moved . . . stood there as before, pointing skyward. The gloom and the rain were now so thick that the hand could no longer be distinguished . . . only the arm reaching up into darkness. [Pp. 77–78]

Nils's sorrow is deepened by his meeting with Per's aged father, who begs him to look after his boy when they get to America. The old man knows that his older son drinks heavily and fears Per will follow his example. He asks Nils to mention his boys every time he writes home. As the steamer heads seaward, Nils glimpses high on a crag of the headland and "square in the face of the westwind storm [. . .] a hunched figure, leaning forward" (p. 81). It is his father, broken in spirit, watching him go—huddled against the cold, surrounded by an immense loneliness.

Though part 1 of *The Boat of Longing* is the work of a mature artist, the rest of the novel is of a markedly inferior quality. It is difficult for Rölvaag to make the switch from Norway to America, from the cove under the hill to Minneapolis. He had written convincingly about rural South Dakota in *Letters from America*, building upon his own experiences as a newcomer; but of immigrant life in urban centers he knew less. His handling of slum life is awkward, and though he recognizes the causes of delinquency, he does not express them believably. There is something of the religious tract about part 2 ("In Foreign Waters"), and most of the characters are merely the "types" which he professes not to believe in.

Almost immediately Nils learns the truth about America's unlimited promise. He first runs up against the language barrier, which keeps him from ever entering fully into life around him. He seeks relief from loneliness in the great crowds which surge through the downtown area "like a Nordland undertow," for it is humanity that interests him most. Not all men are happy in America, Nils discovers; even some faces among the prosperous have a look of "having rowed against the wind all their lives." Nonetheless, his letters home seem like glowing pictures to his parents because he colors drab events to cheer them and sends only good news.

He finds work as janitor in a number of business places, including several saloons. Like Per in *Letters from America*, whose job is cleaning the barn and feedings pigs, Nils becomes less hopeful of a beautiful life. He dislikes especially cleaning the saloons:

> It was most disagreeable on days when he had to wash the places . . . a saloon might become revoltingly filthy after a ribald Saturday night. Nils couldn't understand how people could make such beasts of themselves; they scarcely resembled human beings any longer—no, not even animals. And they were Norwegians, too, many of them. At times he wanted to cry over all the wretchedness he was compelled to witness toward the end of such a Saturday evening. Again and again he would say to himself that he'd never touch strong drink. [P. 97]

It must be admitted that part 2 is strongly propagandistic. At one time early in his career Rölvaag was a lecturer for the Anti-Saloon League in Minnesota, and his own bias is evident. But to suppose as one critic does that Nils's reaction to what he sees in the saloon is unbelievable or unnatural is to fail to understand his temperament.[18] Remembering the home and background from which he comes and the dream that draws him to America, one realizes that his reaction is inevitable. Nor does Nils act prudishly toward Weismann,[19] the alcoholic, when he is reluctant to fetch his bottle from under the bed. The youthful idealist has been wounded by the discovery that this poet, for whom he feels respect and affection, is dying a spiritual death in America. Furthermore, Nils recognizes himself in some aspects of Weismann's personality. He may be ingenuous and naïve in his relations with him, but he is never hypocritical or insincere. It is not to liquor itself that Rölvaag objects in this novel (Nils, after all, drinks a glass of red wine with Kristine Dahl) but to the role of liquor as a factor in immigrant delinquency. It is doubtful, however, that he succeeds in presenting alcohol as one of the forces undermining the establishment of a healthy immigrant society.

In Minneapolis Nils lives in a boarding house occupied by other immigrants—Swedes, Poles, Germans, Irishmen—many of whom cannot speak English, sharing a room with Weismann, a fellow Norwegian. Weismann is a great hulk of a man whose life, dedicated to poetry, represents both achievement and failure. Rölvaag uses him to show that "we're not all bulldog materialists in America, either!" Yet America rejects this poet, this "wise man." It is not enough to say that he ought to be rejected because much of his poetry is bad. What Rölvaag wants us to understand is that Weismann has not had a chance in America. His is the one voice worth hearing in the rooming house called "Babel," but he speaks of concerns foreign to the others, who are dedicated to materialistic pursuits.

Though Rölvaag presents Weismann sympathetically as the rejected artist, he makes it clear that his self-centeredness is the cause of his failure. The poet chastizes Nils for "wearing out shoe leather

18. Stevens, "Rölvaag,," p. 59.
19. The spellings "Weismann" and "Weisman" are both found in the Solum translation of *The Boat of Longing*.

along with the riff-raff on Washington Avenue" when he could have remained more profitably in Weismann's ivory tower, communing with the spirits of great writers, a view of art which Nils does not share. Yet Weismann also gives Nils some good advice: he cautions him to hold fast to the concept of mission in the creative life. Avoid the errors of your fellow immigrants, the poet writes to Nils, and do not lose your soul in pursuit of wealth, ease, and material gains. Eschew gold and fame and catch a vision of a different order. Be like the *askeladd:*

> "That lad saw his own potentialities, that's what he saw! God's deep intention with him. And the eventuality of his finally reaching the castle and winning the princess after incredible difficulties is merely the folk mind's poetic way of expressing an ethical truth. Simply stated, it means that he gained his own soul, his own Self. That's the most which any human being can win! Of such the Lean One will have to keep hands off; God's own good angels will come for them!"
> [P. 146]

Weismann expresses Rölvaag's thoroughly Ibsenian insistence upon the life-integrating ideal, which makes art an ethical as well as esthetic experience. But it takes greater courage than Weismann possesses to stand upright against forces opposing a dedicated life. Nils must see the dangers clearly in order to fight well against them, must be able to answer the question put to him in Weismann's haunting ballad:

> "What are you doing
> In this thin rain,
> Dreaming old memories
> Over again? . . .
>
> This is a fearful place
> When bleak winds call,
> The last crow shivers,
> The last leaves fall."
> [Pp. 146–47]

A chance meeting one day with Kristine Dahl as he skips stones on the Mississippi River and whistles a Nordland tune temporarily tightens the loosening ties with Norway. She is a motherly old woman, from Nordland too, who invites him into her home to share memories of mountain and sea and to speak of their loneliness in the great city. As Nils plays her violin, he relives the experience on the mountain in Norway: his dedication to "the highest" and his decision to go to America. The song he plays is his own "Boat of Longing":

> Before him, in the sublime, lay a wide-stretching sea, drifting in golden calm. Out against the sky-line, sped a boat under bellying sails . . . . Foam broke white around its prow. From aboard came music . . . with laughter in it . . . and crying. It laid itself upon the sun-kissed waters and came rocking toward him.
> . . . The longing to be aboard seized him, filling him with nameless anguish. [P. 115]

He remembers Zalma and home and his yearning for the creative life. "Merciful God," he whispers, "guide my life, so that I may in some measure do what I now feel."

Rölvaag believed that the Norwegian Lutheran Church of America was uniquely able to help Norwegian immigrants achieve spiritual well-being by assisting in the preservation of native cultural values. He soon discovered, however, that many Norwegian-American pastors were themselves culturally adrift, hence unable to understand the needs of their parishioners. The church's failure prompts Weismann to describe for Nils two gentlemen who came to invite him to join their congregation:

> "Dandy apostles, I must say!" Weismann snorted. "Fit envoys to send to such fellows as you and me! And you can guess the burden of their witnessing? No, my son, how could you guess such riddles? Your honest soul is not sufficiently encrusted with hypocrisy. Yes, they said—they said their congregation was a—a—" the Poet cast about for the equivalent expression in Norwegian, but failing to find it, had to employ the English, "a live-ly bunch!" The Poet hiccoughed it out. "Ever hear the likes of that for apostolic tidings?" [P. 213]

## The Peril of Rootlessness

Weismann attacks the indifference and ineffectuality of these "witnesses." True apostles would be animated by a vigorous faith and sense of mission. We note that this incident is completely unmotivated and that Rölvaag, still at times the apprentice, too often uses characters merely as vehicles for ideas.

Part 3 of *The Boat of Longing* takes Nils and Per to a logging camp in northern Minnesota. This section is called "Adrift" to suggest the lethargy into which Nils lapses after struggling to maintain his integrity in a hostile culture. The Foreword refers to this book as "a series of moving pictures," perhaps implying a lack of unity. But it is not a highly impressionistic novel. The problem is that it lacks focus, and part 3 does not serve very well to develop the main themes.

In the woods Nils meets an old Norwegian, a former sailor, who helps renew his faith in the creative life. Value the individual above society, the old man advises—and love humanity. We have failed to do this in our world, and as a result it is composed not of human beings but of types: doctors, lawyers, teachers, farmers. Weismann, the poet, failed partially because he lacked the love and courage necessary to forge onward. But at the age of seventy-two this old woodsman-sailor is heading for Alaska, thence perhaps across the straits to Siberia.

With money in their pockets after the winter's work, Nils and Per get on the train for Minneapolis. Along the way a stranger comes aboard and takes a seat near them. To Per he seems to be the *askeladd* himself, but Nils sees that he is loud, lying, flashy—typical of one aspect of American culture. Just such a stranger appears frequently in Norwegian folk tales as the devil in disguise. Shortly before the train pulls into Minneapolis, Nils dozes off and has a strange dream while Per and his new friend are exchanging confidences. He is back in Norway, far out on the open sea, pulling in halibut lines. Suddenly another boat appears close by in which the stranger, shouting to his companion, Per, is also pulling in lines:

Now their lines got tangled—the stranger's and Nils's. Nils pulled for dear life, till the perspiration poured from him. He meant to have that fish. The stranger pulled equally hard; looked as though he wanted it, too. Just then another great sea rolled in, took the boat from in under and again sent it clean to the sky . . . "Watch out or we'll lock! Slack your line!" shouted Nils. "We'll be dashed to smithers!" [Pp. 196–97]

At that moment Nils is awakened by the conductor's call. Implicit in the dream is his awareness of the struggle for possession of the immigrant's soul. He and the stranger are locked in a battle over Per which threatens to destroy all three of them. When Per disappears with the stranger the next day, it is clear that Nils has failed in his attempt to save him.

Back in Minneapolis Nils himself faces a crisis. Formerly his intense loneliness had been relieved by meetings with Kristine Dahl, the elderly Norwegian woman who had befriended him shortly after his arrival. But she has died during his absence, leaving him one hundred dollars and her violin. She believed that the violin, which belonged originally to her sweetheart, had God's special blessing and was an instrument of good. "You see," she told him once, "only good hands must have it, hands that won't shame it" (p. 155). The violin is a symbol of the continuity that must exist if good is to be transmitted. Nils accepts the violin and the demands upon him which he knows his acceptance entails and at the same time is more keenly aware than ever before of the void in his life. As one critic has remarked, although the irresponsible Per could make an easy adjustment and find satisfaction in material pursuits, "Nils, whose idealism gives him desires that are not so easily satisfied, makes the awful discovery that he has cheated himself. He has only an empty, vulgar life on the edge of things."[20]

The real tragedy for Nils is that he is driven toward a break with the past not by his own wish but by forces beyond his control.

---

20. James Gray, review of *The Boat of Longing*, *St. Paul Dispatch*, February 1, 1933.

# The Peril of Rootlessness

Otto and Per have no connections with Norway; they willingly cut them when they left in order to drift unfettered in America. Nils, however, treasures the ties with the homeland. But because he cannot be encouraging about Per and Otto, he puts off writing letters to his parents, though he needs the reassurance their replies bring.

How deeply Nils is disturbed by Per's leaving with the stranger is shown by a dream he has one evening as he dozes in the railway station. He is on a mountain top—as he had been once before at Væröy when he dedicated his life to music—looking out over an utterly desolate landscape. But he is impelled to descend into the dismal valley below. The most horrible part of the dream is the luminous eyes of Ole Hansen, shining far off in the darkness. Nils trembles and prays they will not find him out, dreading their silent rebuke for his failure to save Per and Otto. The way down the mountain is perilous, and at the bottom lie bleached bones. Through this valley Nils must walk, taking care that his own bones never rest there, rotting in the pale, sulphurous light. Nils's vision represents Rölvaag's conviction that the artist must eagerly embrace life in all of its phases, not live in retreat as Weismann does. He must be aware too of life in the depths, where all that is evil lurks.

This dream ends part 3. The last word we have of Nils is that he spends the following two years in a railroad crew:

> Happening to get into a city of a Saturday night, he would immediately seek out the city's busiest corner; and there he would stand searching and searching, like a lone gull perched watchful on some bold headland round which the ocean current runs swift.
>
> Those really becoming aware of the face were involuntarily made to wonder at its sad and weary look, especially since it seemed so young. [P. 243]

Thus, Nils's story ends with his irrevocable commitment, even in the face of powerful odds, to try to understand humanity and preserve the individual personality in a society which perceives men as types only. But Rölvaag has not finished with the third of the three major themes: the cost of immigration to those who remain behind. In part 4 ("Hearts That Ache") the story returns to Norway, where Nils's parents and Ole Hansen await word of their sons. It is two years since Nils last wrote, and the old people are sad and anxious. Ole suggests a trip to America to try to find out what happened. The idea frightens Jo, who has never left his native shore, but, timid and withdrawn though he is, he nerves himself to go. He and Anna visit the pastor to receive communion and ask God's blessing on his trip.

On his arrival in New York Jo is not permitted to land because he does not have a letter from his son guaranteeing his support. The shock and disappointment are devastating, and he thenceforth lives entirely in a dream world. On the ship returning to Norway, he meets an old Norwegian woman who tells him tales of wondrous America. She had been unhappy while visiting in Minnesota and is eager to be back in her cotter's hut, alone in familiar surroundings. For six weeks she lived with her sons in Duluth, but it was not like home:

> [I]t had seemed lonesome and queer not to be able to talk to the children of her boys, those blessed children that were so pretty and who were in a way her own.
> —Couldn't she talk to them? To her son's children?—Unable to comprehend, Jo had to question further.
> —No, for they couldn't, of course, talk Norwegian!
> Couldn't they talk Norwegian? Her own children's children?
> —Again Jo failed to understand. [P. 293]

She had visited Minneapolis with one of her sons and lived with many other people in "a large house with thick carpets," obviously a hotel. Yes, she answers Jo's query, she surely saw someone in the same house who fitted the description of Nils: of medium height, broad-shouldered, blond, blue-eyed. In this knowledge Jo takes refuge. At home Anna is entranced, yet troubled, by his fairy-tale account of Nils's life in America, aware of an unnatural brightness in his eyes. On the evening of his return, he rows out to sea—toward Nils's beautiful castle in the west—and is never seen again.

## The Peril of Rootlessness

In spite of the high quality of much of the writing in *The Boat of Longing*, several serious flaws prevent its being an entirely successful novel: the awkward transition from Norway to America; the inadequate presentation of problems of urban life and the language of the streets; and the unreality of the evil which Nils encounters in the big city. We are not, for example, strongly moved by a sense of the depravity of the prostitutes, as Rölvaag intended us to be, finding neither pathos nor despair in their condition. We are troubled by the lack of integration of the north woods interval and a discrepancy in the conception of at least one of the main characters, Kristine Dahl. She is first presented as an old woman, wrinkled and slow on her feet. Coming back after a winter in the woods, Nils wonders if she will still be alive; yet she seems to have been a young woman when her betrothed was drowned in the storm of 1893. Since the time of the novel is about 1911, she actually must be under fifty years of age and is perhaps even in her late thirties.

In spite of these weaknesses, and partly because of the sensitive translation by Nora Solum, *The Boat of Longing* is full of life. We note especially the ring of truth in the best dialogue; the superb characterizations of Nils, Jo, and Mother Anna; the pathos of the peasant notion that America is a fairyland across the sea; and the convincing violation of Nils's innocence.

Rölvaag had now prepared the way for his masterpiece, *Giants in the Earth*. Although the two novels are not organically related, *The Boat of Longing* anticipates *Giants in the Earth* both chronologically and artistically. The latter book, as George W. Spohn observes, depicts the life of the immigrant pitting himself against the elemental forces of nature to wrest a living from the untamed prairie; while the former recreates an earlier stage of this westward movement, the immigrant's departure from the motherland and the initial impacts of and adjustments to the new world.[21]

---

21. Spohn, review of *The Boat of Longing* (see note 13, above).

# 5

# THE COST
# OF THE SETTLEMENT:
## giants in the earth

*I*n the spring of 1923 Rölvaag learned that the Norwegian novelist
Johan Bojer was planning a trip to the United States to investigate
Norwegian immigration preliminary to writing a novel which would
present the first adequate portrayal of his people's role in settling
America.[1] Rölvaag had long believed that this story ought to be
told and that he himself was the man to tell it. Although the
settling of the West had been accomplished before his arrival, his
years on the farm in Elk Point had acquainted him with at least
some of the settlers' problems, either through his own experiences
or through the tales of homesteaders still living in the area, and he
understood the fundamental issue for the novelist who wrote of
the Norwegian pioneers: the psychological and spiritual conflict
into which they were plunged.

Believing that he must work full time on the novel, Rölvaag
requested a leave of absence from St. Olaf College for the year
1923–24. He intended to spend part of this period in the northern
Minnesota wilderness, where it would be possible to approximate
the primitive conditions of pioneer life. During the summer of
1922 he had built a vacation cabin near Marcell, Itasca County,
Minnesota, about 270 miles from Northfield in the woods along
Big Island Lake. Mrs. Rölvaag writes that such a retreat had to
front upon water:

---

1. Bojer's work, *Vor Egen Stamme* [*Our Own Folk*] (Christiania, 1924), was
published several weeks after Book I of *Giants in the Earth* appeared in Norway.
The following year it appeared in an English edition with the title *The
Emigrants*, trans. by A. G. Jayne (New York: Century Co. [1925]).

As a child he played in the boats that lay at anchor below the home; as a young lad he had his first lessons in fishing with his father and elder brother in the home waters; as a young man from the age of fourteen to twenty (when he emigrated to America) he was a Lofot fisherman. Even we who know little if anything about that sort of life must understand how deeply he missed it. Always he longed for the sea.[2]

Two sites had appealed strongly to the family: the shore of Big Ole Lake, facing west, commanding a fine view of the sunset; and the shore of Big Island Lake, from which they could watch the sunrise over the water. Rölvaag chose the Big Island site, and with the help of friends cleared and began building. On July 11, 1922, the family moved into the cottage.

Rölvaag now had secured his vacation home, a cozy and peaceful place where he could work undisturbed. No telephone—no daily paper—no radio. Only occasionally might a guest from some nearby resort pass by or the neighbors come in for a short visit.

The porch became Rölvaag's study. From his work table here, he had the best view of the lake. Did it remind him of the sea and the homeland? Perchance it eased, in a small measure, that deep longing for the bigger sea. This too was a water where one could sit in a boat and dream while he fished. I am positive that many of the problems he had with his characters were solved on Big Island Lake! "For characters in a book are just like other ordinary human beings," he would often say. They were not always willing to do his bidding. At times he had to struggle hard with them. Then it was well he could be with them alone and undisturbed. Rölvaag never talked much about his work, but I could tell when he was deep in it. He might be so preoccupied as scarcely to notice what went on around him. One day when he came in from the lake he remarked, "Well, now, I've finally got Beret to behave!"

---

2. Quoted from a paper read by Mrs. O. E. Rölvaag to Idun Edda, a Norwegian society at St. Olaf College, in 1942. Translated from the Norwegian. The four quotations following are from the same source.

# The Cost of the Settlement

Mrs. Rölvaag describes their life at the cabin. After breakfast, Rölvaag generally retired to his study on the porch, where he wrote until about eleven o'clock. Then it was time for exercise, usually clearing the woods or chopping firewood. Just before the noon meal the family went for a swim. While the children were washing the dishes, Rölvaag rested, his wife reading aloud:

> Many books were read during those rest periods. It did happen quite frequently that he dozed off and I stopped reading. "Go on," he would grunt, half asleep.
> "But you were sleeping."
> "Continue your reading."
> And I read, for this I enjoyed doing.

After the rest period it was time for a cup of coffee and perhaps another swim. Back at the work table, he was often busy until sunset. On days when the weather was agreeable, they often took a little fishing trip just before dark, when the fish had moved in to feed near shore. On those occasions supper would be late, perhaps at nine o'clock. During the evenings Rölvaag was busy with his extensive correspondence:

> They were the coziest, most intimate part of the day. Then we gathered around the big table, where the old Aladdin lamp from school days threw its cheerful beams, each one busy with his own interest. When Rölvaag laid down his pen, we might take a walk down to the pier to watch the fish splash in the water, or the stars' reflection. Or when the moon was bright, row far out and imagine ourselves in a charmed fairyland.
>
> When cold or rainy days came, we simply moved into the cabin. The crackling of the popple burning in the old wood range, accompanied by the drip, drip of the rain on the roof, and the cheerful glow of the lamp made the room a friendly retreat. The world with its problems was completely shut out. Such an atmosphere might inspire anyone to write.

Fishing trips on Big Island Lake sometimes took them into primitive wilderness areas. One favorite spot was in North Bay, an almost hidden arm joining a larger body of water:

Here a dense forest surrounds the cove, giving it a dark and unnatural cast. One could easily imagine trolls and goblins lurking among the trees. In such a desolate region we felt ourselves completely shut out from the rest of the world. No sign of life anywhere—only the beaver working diligently on the shore.

Though Rölvaag undoubtedly had been thinking about his pioneer novel during most of the summer of 1923, we know that he did not begin its composition until after July 20, on which date he wrote to a friend that he had "not written a word yet."[3] On August 30 Mrs. Rölvaag and the children set out by train to visit her parents in Sioux Falls, South Dakota. Rölvaag planned to devote himself to intensive writing during their absence. At the beginning of his stay alone he had a draft of the opening chapters only; in the eight weeks that followed he completed a rough sketch of the entire novel.

Excerpts from letters to his wife during those weeks present a picture of his progress and occasionally of his moods. In later years he often said that the novel could never have been written had he not experienced the solitude and loneliness of that stay in the wilderness. A reader familiar with *Giants in the Earth* will understand the importance of the questions he asks his father-in-law, Andrew Berdahl, and will be able to follow the progress of the novel through such incidents as the coming of the Indians, the birth and baptism of Peder Victorious, the arrival of the insane woman, and the grasshopper plague. The letters also provide an account of his work habits and reveal his confidence that this novel would have no equal of its kind in fiction. The first letter, dated August 31, 1923, tells of his activities since leaving his family in Deer River the preceding day:

> [This morning] I wrote for an hour and a half, until dinner time. I had boiled potatoes and the ham that was left over but no coffee. We had a heavy rain while I was writing. After

---

3. Rölvaag to Waldemar Ager, July 20, 1923. Copy in the Rölvaag Collection.

dinner I washed dishes, swept the floor, and took my rifle for a little trip toward the north. I went as far as the road to Club House [Lake] but saw nothing. I made coffee when I got back about three. Now I have written for an hour and a half. Before going to bed I shall write two more hours. That will make five hours today and that should be enough. If I can do four sections each day, I am doing well. Right now I am writing about Indians.[4]

[September 5, 1923.] But now you must get the following information from Grandfather. And I should have it as soon as possible. It concerns the settling itself:

(1) Where was the land office for the whole stretch between Sioux Falls and Brookings about 1873?

(2) Had the government put down markers for each quarter in 1873? Or only for each section?

(3) When a man filed in the fall, what kind of markers did he place on the quarter he chose for himself? (I presume that he moved onto that land the following spring.) Ask him to describe such a marker for you.

[September 8, 1923.] Yesterday I wrote all forenoon and a while in the afternoon, but today I have written nothing. I realize that I am not able to do more than four hours of creative work. When I begin to rewrite, I shall manage eight. That is so *much, much* easier.

Please greet Grandfather and say that his last notes are absolutely priceless! Just what I needed. If I produce a good book from this, the least honor from it will not be his. When I give a dramatic picture of what he has been telling, people will have to take notice or I miss my guess. That was fine! I really should be chatting with him each evening now in order to create a more realistic atmosphere. Please ask him the following questions and write me so that he need not do it:

(1) Where was the filing office for the whole prairie country between Sioux Falls and Brookings in 1873? Or was there more than one place? If so, where?

---

4. Excerpts from Rölvaag's letters have been translated from the Norwegian unless otherwise indicated.

(2) Did it ever happen that one person filed for another? In other words, did a man *have* to appear in person in order to file, or could someone do it for him?

(3) If a man filed in the fall but could not settle before the following spring, was it customary in such cases that the man went out to the piece of land he had filed on and put down some kind of marker?

(4) Ask him if he remembers hearing about any mixups in filing and consequent contests. (I have heard of some from Goodhue County, Minnesota, but of course, that was much earlier.)

(5) I would like also very much to find out what year Madison and Lake Preston were founded.

(6) The time between filing and settling, that is, before establishing abode, could not be over six months, could it?

There are perhaps other things I shall need to straighten out, but they can wait until later, perhaps until I come. His information is, as I have said, absolutely priceless. However, it is remarkable how this came to me intuitively. It is not far from the truth as it is. But his narrative gives me so much more assurance, and that gives power, as you can see.

[September 12, 1923.] Today I have written much. I think I shall manage six thousand words before I retire, and that is much more than usual for even the world's great writers. Four thousand is a really good day's work. Both yesterday and Monday were good days but not so good as today. Hope I may continue this way for a few weeks.

[September 14, 1923.] I rewrote a chapter this forenoon, and this evening I shall take it up again. Have something very difficult to work out: about a birth on the Dakota prairie in the winter of 1873 and the baptism of that child at home. A good theme, all right, but difficult to handle to the satisfaction of our prudish Puritans.

That reminds me of your last information. If the filing office was at Vermillion, how could they file? Grandfather has never told me that they came near Vermillion, and surely all who took land were not there. Now these are just the points:

(1) Did a man have to appear in person in order to file, or

could friends or relatives do it for him? Part of my plot hinges on *this one thing*.

(2) Does Grandfather know of cases where people settled *first* and filed *afterwards?*

After I get this straight I don't think I shall need him before I get to Sioux Falls.

Grandfather is of inestimable value to me in this work—he and my own experience up here in this wilderness. I could scarcely have written the book if I had not had some intimate glimpses of pioneer life up here. This is fate again, you see. This work will be entirely unlike any of my other books. But I think I am doing pretty well. If only the oldtimers will read it! In places it is completely realistic, I believe.

[September 16, 1923.] I now have 102 pages of rough sketch, 72 since you left. That should make at least 300 pages rewritten. By Thursday evening I shall have finished the sketch of the whole first volume. There will be two volumes, but they will be published simultaneously. At any rate, I shall write the whole thing in one go-round.This is the first time I have finished the sketch of the entire work first, and I believe it has many advantages. We shall see. Yes, I am sure now that I shall produce a good book. It will be my masterpiece, so I hope. If only I can have patience to continue this way until I finish the entire preliminary sketch! I don't expect soon again to do as well as I did last week when I managed about 30,000 words. That is *well done*. Much of it is also in such good shape that it needs only to be copied.

[September 20, 1923.] I am satisfied with the manuscript. The historical aspect of it is right just as I have it; however, I shall ask Grandfather to check that part.

[September 25, 1923.] This week I have not written so rapidly as last, but I have written well, that I know.

[October 3, 1923.] Now it is 4:30 and I have worked steadily since 9:30 with barely an hour off for lunch. [. . .] Today I wrote about the grasshoppers, and if I can portray it as I feel it, the incident will be very well done.

[October 5, 1923.] I need more information from Grandfather. Here are the questions (answer each one briefly):

(1) How many acres per day could be reaped with the reaper Grandfather had?

(2) How many horses did it require?

(3) When was the first religious service held in that neighborhood? In what year?

(4) Who was the pastor that conducted them?

(5) Where did the pastor live then?

(6) In what part of the summer did Grandfather return from Elk Point from the Territorial Convention?

[October 8, 1923.] Yesterday I was alone all day at home and wrote almost the whole time. It was one of my best days. Today also I have done well, but not so well as yesterday.

The day has been cloudy with occasional raindrops and strong wind. A few leaves still remain, mostly on the poplars. Strange how tough these leaves are. But today many have been blown down. One can scarcely imagine how different the countryside is with the leaves falling. Almost like another landscape. The land is so flat. It is still lovely but lonesome. All those pale poplar leaves on those pale branches! An eerie sight, but very, very lovely. [. . .] I feel that I should stay here longer. There is no place in the world where I can work better or with less interruption than here.

[October 12, 1923.] I have decided not to drive myself so hard and am slowing down. During the past two weeks I have written no more than five or six hours per day. Even so, I have put together much good stuff. [. . .] I know I am doing a great work. I can already tell that I shall turn out a piece of art that will make anyone bearing my name feel mighty proud of it. Not all of our people will like it. The book may even fall flat, but this I do *know!* that it will stand comparison with anything else that has been produced in this country and elsewhere during the last decade. You have never heard me so positive about any of my books before, have you? Well, my own feeling may prove wrong as to the reception of the work. That, however, is a minor matter. I know that the book shall have lasting value.

[October 19, 1923.] It is almost 5:00 p.m. and I have worked faithfully since 7:30 this morning; so you see I am not taking it easy. I have worked all day with a woman who cannot endure the loneliness of the prairie—a good theme but not easy to manage so that it seems believable. But she will serve her purpose, wait and see!

[October 21, 1923.] Snow fell last night, and it was cold and clear. [. . .] We drove in the Ford down [to our hunting spot], arriving just at daybreak. Fog lay thick and white over the water. I tell you, it was beautiful to see the morning glow spreading over the mist and the snow lying on the pines and firs. Well, I got no ducks, froze like a dog, and was soaking wet—but that didn't matter. Wish you had been with me on that point, watching daylight flood the horizon—a sight worth everything! [. . .] Now as I sit here thinking about the beauty I have seen today in this wonderfully rare and desolate landscape—water, sun, clear sky, bare trees, evergreens—I feel that I have spent a blessed Sunday in God's great cathedral. [. . .] And this I know: tomorrow I can work! I believe I can write for six hours without even breathing!

And now the new moon rises over Big Island, peering so queerly at me between the bare trees, glistening on the branches, where snow crystals still nestle. A thousand goodnights! Hurrah for bed!

[October 22, 1923.] It is 3:00 p.m. here in the cabin. I have written steadily since early morning and now am tired and want to chat with you awhile. I shall work a little this evening so I'll have a long day nevertheless. [. . .] I shall break up my solitary life at the cabin early Saturday morning, November 3. I am longing powerfully for you and the children. And still, leaving makes me sad. I have seen the moon grow and light up these lakes and woods four times. I can't say which was more beautiful: the moon bathing the summer in light, or shining upon a bare, gray autumn landscape.

[October 26, 1923.] Yes, a week from this evening I shall have everything packed, ready to leave the next morning. Do you know, it will be sad to leave? It has been lonely at times—dreadfully lonely—but mostly because I longed for you and the children. [. . .] My pen has done well this last week. Though I'm not working fast, this is the best writing I have ever done. The book grows thrilling with life. It is glorious to sit this way and create human souls and knit them together. I doubt that any joy can compare with that which an artist feels.

Rölvaag left Marcell on November 3 to join his family at Sioux Falls, but his stay with them was brief. On September 3 the St. Olaf College chapel had burned down and a new building was needed immediately. Because of increased enrollment and expansion of the curriculum, officials decided to build an administration-classroom building instead of a chapel. Although he was on leave, Rölvaag offered his services to the college. He arrived in Northfield on November 19 and spent the next few weeks soliciting contributions from Norwegian-Lutheran congregations in South Dakota, southern Minnesota, and Wisconsin.

Shortly after the first of the year he arranged a trip to Norway, where he hoped to finish his novel and find a publisher. On February 7, he left New York City, and after a week's stay in England arrived in Oslo February 25. There he took a room in a private home and settled down to complete his work. Letters to his family in Sioux Falls indicate weariness as he completes the task of filling in the rough sketch:

[March 27, 1924.] This week has been peaceful and quiet; I've done nothing but work. But though I have tried hard, I haven't progressed very fast. However, I believe I am achieving something good. I am entirely finished with Book I and am well on the way with Book II. At the moment I am picturing a woman whom loneliness and adversity drove insane out in the Dakota Territory in the beginning of the seventies. It is intensely interesting. If I can achieve what I have in mind, my novel will show what it all cost, the wealth and beauty there in the West. [. . .] I hope this letter finds you well and in good spirits. The latter is almost the most important. Everything depends on courage, which contributes to good health, and both you and I have so much to live for. Right now I feel my purpose in life more strongly than ever before. And this I know, *that* purpose I can never achieve unless you help me. Perhaps you can't help me with the actual work, but you can do so very much by helping me in other ways. And if you do that will have a real part in my work also. Prestige doesn't matter; what matters is to be faithful!

[March 31, 1924.] I sent you a letter at noon today. There was a sad note in it so now I am sending a few more words which I hope will be better. There were two reasons for my bad mood: All last week I wrote about a dark and tragic episode and at last became completely despondent myself. Then too I went about thinking of you, and when no letter came, my spirits sank even lower.

[April 14, 1924.] I am writing to you this evening because the morning hours, from ten o'clock until two, are the best work hours; I don't want to be disturbed then if I can help it. [. . .] This week I have been faithful as the proverbial ant and feel certain that I have worked harder than any other St. Olaf teacher. But if anything will come of it, only the Lord knows. I have written much and am well along in the second part of the novel. However, I am not as optimistic as I was last fall. This I do know: It far surpasses anything done up until now among Norwegian-Americans.

[April 21, 1924.] Lately I have worked very hard—very, very hard. I think I shall reconsider and stay here until I have finished the book, which should be about June 1. The advantage of this plan is that I can work in peace until it is completed. Going to a new place would mean an unfortunate interruption. It might be that then I could go north and have a real vacation.

Last night my landlady invited me to a cod dinner at nine o'clock. What good coffee! It was a fine meal, and I wrote until almost two o'clock this morning—good writing. Yes, this I know: I have worked this year and that is the truth!

[April 28, 1924.] Life is an awful business when everything is said and done. May you never know the darkness of despair that sometimes has enveloped me! and still does surround me. But I am gradually working out of it.[5]

[May 4, 1924.] A publisher in Norway for Norwegian-American literature is simply impossible. Didn't realize before how

---

5. Written in English.

impossible it is. If the picture drawn is true to our life in the West, people here couldn't understand it, because they cannot see that we have come to be a different people from them. Hence the book wouldn't sell. I am, however, going to let one publisher look through my Ms, but that will be all; there isn't a ghost of a show that he will care to take it. Such is life, and there you are. I am not feeling bad about it![6]

[May 12, 1924.] Today is Monday, and exactly two weeks from today I shall go to Nordland. And in two weeks I shall have nearly finished the book. Probably not entirely but almost. You can't imagine how hard I have worked. I can say without boasting that I have been diligent. In the form used here, it will be a work of about 600 printed pages, and all that I have done since you left me up in the woods. Between November 15 and March 1 there was hardly any writing; you can see from that that I have been busy.

Have no idea what the book will be like. Again, as before with my work, when the end approaches I become very dissatisfied with the whole thing. [. . .] Well, well, if it were only finished because now I am dreadfully tired.

[May 21, 1924.] One day this spring I visited the publisher-in-chief of Aschehougs Forlag, the largest publishing house in Norway, and told him that I was writing a lengthy pioneer novel and asked if they would be interested in seeing the manuscript. He said they were but gave me little hope. [. . .] When I was so far along that only ninety pages remained unfinished, I took the part that was ready to the chief. When he learned that I didn't have all of it, he wanted to wait, since the ending is always very important in a book. I got a little warm under the collar and told him that the publisher who wouldn't accept or reject the manuscript as it was, wasn't worth salt in the soup. So then he took it. I didn't hear from him until last night. When I got home there was a letter from the chief, asking me for an interview in his office, and I was there today.

Yes, the reviewer has recommended that they take the manuscript! So far so good. First of all that will take some time; then too it will cost me about 350 kroner, at least fifty dollars. Then too I need to work way up to the middle of July since

---

6. Written in English.

there are many little things I would like to change and would need to change even if the book didn't come out here. This I had planned to do in odd moments and also on my way back over the ocean. If I let the publishers here have it, I shall have to be at Nordland until the middle of July and then come back here and stay a month—at least three weeks—while I get it "hammered" on the machine.

Now there is only one hitch in all this. The book will be quite expensive. In the chief's office today we figured that the two-volume set will cost about twenty-five kroner here, about $3.25 in America. This causes me considerable anxiety; you see I lack confidence in myself. Well, then, I have no need to worry over the price. That is true, but it would be too bad if the publishers should lose money on me. That would spoil everything for the poor Norwegian-American writers who might follow me. That is why I dread the responsibility.

[May 28, 1924.] So far, this trip [on the fjord-boat] has been very enjoyable. Since coming aboard I have worked quite diligently. Have read the first twenty pages and made quite a few changes. Hope they are an improvement.

[June 4, 1924.] Yes, now I am sitting by the familiar window in the old living room of the ancient homestead; and I look down upon the cove called Rölvaag to the sea and the birds; and across to the mountain ridges and bare islands beyond; and I hear children speaking this curious language, so droll as it comes from their mouths, so melodiously melancholy as spoken by their elders. As I sit here *seeing* and *hearing*, I am in reality only a vessel of sensations that has suddenly opened up to drink in all impressions with a thirsty mouth; and a mixed mood comes over me. I am happy and could sing—but am also sad; now, for the first time, I realize that I am a ghost from the past. Not only do my impressions of nature witness to that; even more do I sense the separation in the many changes since I was last here. There are new people, an unbelievably large group of them; human life is fruitful in these otherwise barren places. There is many a new shelter for both man and animal—and many a new boat! All is new. Even the folks who once were close to me are new in that they have aged so much. This is part of the pilgrim's tragedy; he returns to the old homestead, meets his own flesh and blood, and finds them strangers.

Now you must not think I am disappointed. On the contrary, I am radiantly happy. I came here yesterday in a little sailboat with my two brothers; I sat at the rudder myself. The sea was high—quite a storm blowing—and we had no oilskins. The result was that all three of us were as wet from head to foot as if we had been ducked. I changed at once and feel not even a sniffle today. Last night I slept like a stone, and now my heart is beating entirely normally again.

[June 14, 1924.] Every afternoon I write and have now sent one-third of the manuscript to a typist in Christiania [Oslo]. A week from today I shall have finished most of it.

[June 17, 1924.] Here is my program now: I fish a little each night, and during the day I work on the manuscript. Today I toiled a good eight hours, arising at six o'clock. When I finish seventy or eighty pages, I send them to the typist in Christiania. Today I sent off eighty-five pages. Hope sincerely that I earn enough through the book to get back my investment. I am still not sure about giving it to the publishers here, but likely I shall. I am dreadfully afraid of the critics in Norway.

[June 30, 1924.] What days! What nights! You have never seen anything like it! Last week we had glorious weather both day and night, absolutely wonderful! This barren landscape has an extravagance of color that is beyond description. It is like a person with an ugly face that has all the world's love in his soul.

Exactly two weeks from today I must break away. The stay has been too short—or too long—no, exactly right. This time I am not eager to leave Rölvaag, for I know that it is the last time I shall see Father and perhaps others, too. [. . .] I shall just barely finish with the manuscript before arriving in Christiania. There I shall proofread it in typed form.

[July 14, 1924.] If the weather was bad and the Nordland sea bade me a harsh welcome, it is now repaying me with a wonderful farewell. It is eight o'clock in the evening, the sea a mirror of untold colors, changing constantly. Magic is in the air and in the land. All is beauty, a beauty completely captivating.

And now I have bidden farewell to Father, to Rölvaag, to sea and home, to Mother's grave, to the ancient fatherland! My heart is heavy tonight. I believe I could scarcely endure another such trip. It is heart-rending. Heartstrings are breaking.

[July 31, 1924.] Something went wrong this time. I should have been in the middle of the Atlantic; instead I am only seven hours from Bergen on the way to England. Undoubtedly you have read in the papers about the fire aboard the "Bergensfjord" and know the reason for my not arriving as soon as expected. [. . .] I worked dreadfully hard on the manuscript the week I was in Christiania, sitting on the same chair sixteen hours out of twenty-four. So you know that I was driving myself. I left it with Aschehoug but haven't too much faith that they will accept it. The last chapters were strongly religious, which people here think is sentimental and don't like. However, I know that I have produced my best book. It is much more distinctive than any other literary effort of mine. And now that I am finished with it, I don't care how things go hereafter. For me there is reward enough in having done it. It is a remarkable work. Running to about six hundred pages, it has been written in different parts of the world: in northern Minnesota, while I was alone at the cabin by day and night; in Sioux Falls, while I pottered about; on the Atlantic Ocean; in a shabby hotel room in London; in hotels in Norway; on boats along Norway's coast; a little bit here and a little bit there. Yet, I believe the book has unity.

The novel was accepted by Aschehoug and published in two parts, the first, entitled *I de Dage: Fortælling om Norske Nykommere i Amerika (In Those Days: A Story of Norwegian Immigrants in America)*, appearing in the fall of 1924; the second volume, *I de Dage: Riket Grundlægges (In Those Days: The Founding of the Kingdom)*, following in 1925. Rölvaag was immediately hailed by Scandinavian critics as a writer of first importance.[7]

---

7. Several typical Scandinavian reviews are quoted in Julius Olson, "Rölvaag's Novels of Pioneer Life in the Dakotas," *Scandinavian Studies and Notes* 12 (August, 1926): 45–55.

Back at his teaching duties at St. Olaf College, he had little time to work on an English translation of the book. Fortunately, an article about him in the *Minneapolis Journal,* January 31, 1926, attracted the attention of Lincoln Colcord, a journalist and short-story writer and a personal friend of Eugene Saxton of Harpers and other men in the publishing field. Colcord, who was then living in Minneapolis, was eager to visit Rölvaag and learn more about his work. Their first meeting resulted in a preliminary plan for the translation of *Giants in the Earth,*[8] and Colcord began his campaign to present Rölvaag's novels to American readers in English-language editions.

Colcord came from an old New England sailing family—had, in fact, spent much of his youth with his father on the China Sea—and the love of sailing and fishing which both men shared was undoubtedly basic to their warm friendship. Colcord wrote enthusiastically to Saxton describing their first meeting:

> [March 9, 1926.] I spent yesterday afternoon with Prof. Rölvaag; the experience was one of the most interesting I've ever had. These are a few of the facts and impressions which I gained.
>
> First, about translations. This situation is in better shape than I feared. There is already in existence a manuscript translation of the first of the two books which you have: *In Those Days.* This is the one which could stand alone; the second volume could not stand without the other. This translation has been carefully revised by Rölvaag and his wife, and is now in the hands of friends for further revision. He will have it back by the first of April, and will be able to submit it to you shortly afterwards.
>
> Regarding the matter of further translations, there is only one man, he tells me, who in his opinion is capable of the work;

---

8. The complicated story of the multiple-translator system which produced *Giants in the Earth* under the supervision of Rölvaag and Lincoln Colcord has been told in Jorgenson and Solum, *Rölvaag,* pp. 364 ff. The Rölvaag-Colcord letters, written mostly between 1926 and 1928, give a clear picture of the progress of the translation and also furnish interesting biographical information.

a friend who teaches in some nearby city. This friend has promised to undertake a translation of the second volume which you have, and will deliver the manuscript by the first of August. A year ago Rölvaag had entered into a contract with Jesse [*sic*] Muir of England, the translator of Bojer's works, to do *In Those Days* into English; when suddenly her physician ordered her to cease all work with her eyes—she was going blind. He feels this stroke of ill-luck deeply.

By far the most important fact I learned was that Rölvaag has written three other novels, and a fourth book of a series of letters recounting the experiences of an emigrant, done as a piece of fiction. The books you have are really his fifth and sixth published works of fiction. The other four were published in Norwegian by the Augsburg Publishing Company of this city, the center of publishing in the Norwegian language here; two of them have reached a circulation of 5,000 each among the Norwegian-speaking people of this region. All this was a great mistake, of course; his life has been full of errors of judgment, as we would say. He sees it clearly now. The publishing of these books in Norwegian here caused them to be looked on with disfavor by publishers in Norway; hence it is only with the last two books, which were not first published here, that he has been able to break through the circle of error. Yet it all came about naturally, in the development of a lonely life without friends or advisers at critical moments.

Rölvaag himself is a powerful personality. He is the short, thick-set, fighting type, and I can see that he has fought for every inch of his life and artistic achievement. He is now a man of fifty, quite disillusioned, calm and serene, and yet still full of vitality and the passion of creative impulse. He is quite decidedly a ripened personality. Whether his work is to be received in English or not, he is entirely confident of its artistic worth. He talks like a man who has paid too heavy a price to be in doubt any longer. He is simple, direct, and fundamental, and without a trace of self-consciousness, a man who would compel interest in any gathering. One knows that he has had a deep and broad experience of life. He is married and has two children living. Two more children died tragically; the oldest, a boy of great artistic promise, died suddenly of some natural cause; the youngest, whom he describes as the most beautiful child he had ever seen, fell into a neighbor's well and was found there drowned after a long search. You know what these things mean. I have come away from the meeting greatly sobered. I feel that I have had an insight into a life of creative genius, of lonliness [*sic*] and adversity, and of unswerving fidelity to an artistic ideal. The books which antedate the ones that have made a name for him, are the more intimate revelations of his own spiritual experience. As he described them to me, I cannot but feel that they will prove to be the greater books in the end. He himself is quite confident of their inherent literary worth. At any rate, you will see from all this that there is a formidable background to the present picture, and a body of work already in existence sufficient to make or break a literary reputation.

He tells me that never before in his life has he been met on just this ground, or felt himself in touch with the publishing profession in America. Doesn't this seem incredible? Such is the lot of the alien in our midst. He simply has had no contacts; and pride no doubt has caused him to lean over backwards in refusing to take ordinary steps. He is very much that type of man.

One other thing, before I close. There can be no doubt of the profound impression made in Norway by Rölvaag's last books. They will soon have to go into a fourth edition. I saw personal letters from some of the most distinguished names in Norwegian literature, all in enthusiastic praise. Rölvaag has been to Norway, has visited at Bojer's house, etc. It is being said that he is creating a new Norwegian language, in his free idiomatic use of the Norwegian-American phraseology. In classical passages, the power of his style is spoken of with wonder by the critics; how can a man who has lived abroad thirty years, teaching in another language, write such Norwegian, it is asked.

He sprang from a family of fishermen on the north coast of Norway. He landed in South Dakota at the age of twenty with a few pennies in his pocket. He earned every cent for his education at farm and factory labor. He retains in a rare way the viewpoint of a man with both feet flat on the ground—smokes a cigar to the very butt, swears fluently, and is chiefly interested in the elements of life. At the same time he has acquired much of the college professor, a certain sternness and precision of mind along with his boyishness. He has been teaching literature for twenty years; just now he is about the country speaking in a campaign to raise funds for St. Olaf's College.

But the story of his life is a long and fascinating one. You would be impressed with it. I hope you will hear it from him some day. I sincerely hope that this isn't to be a flash in the pan.[9]

Harpers decided to publish the novel in one volume as *Giants in the Earth*, a title suggested by Eugene Saxton and taken from the Biblical epigraph which supplied the title for the Norwegian edition: "There were giants in the earth in those days" (Genesis 6:4). The giants of the title are frequently assumed to be Per Hansa and his kind among the early settlers, remembered for their strength and heroism. But the term is tantalizingly ambiguous, considering its Biblical context. The giants of Genesis are superhuman, children of God's sons and the daughters of men—monstrous creatures like the giants of classical mythology or even, at their worst, the trolls of Germanic folklore. They appear in the Old Testament account as a sign of increasing wickedness on earth. Rölvaag's conception of the prairie as a brooding troll and his numerous references to magic and other elements of folklore are evidence that he intended the giants in the earth to be the hostile powers confronting the pioneers: storm, plague, drought, prairie fire, hunger, greed, dread, loneliness. Like the folk heroes of old, Per Hansa and his fellows must do combat with these giants, risking their very souls in the battle. And no mortal escapes unscathed from an encounter with the trolls.

The novel appeared in June of 1927 as a Book of the Month Club selection and was an immediate success, selling almost eighty thousand copies before the end of the year. Typical of the praise accorded Rölvaag is Carl Sandburg's reaction:

---

9. Lincoln Colcord to Eugene Saxton, March 9, 1926. Copy in the Rölvaag Collection.

At St. Olaf's College in Northfield, Minnesota, we met O. E. Rölvaag, author of the novel, *Giants in the Earth*. He is a quiet spoken man, unassuming as a winter landscape. He does not look as though he carries in his heart and breast the immense play of storm and fate unrolled on the scroll of his majestic book. We have had laughter and tears, going from chapter to chapter of *Giants in the Earth*. If we should be asked to name six most important and fascinating American novels past and present, *Giants in the Earth* would be one of them. It is so tender and simple. It is so terrible and panoramic, piling up its facts with incessantly subtle intimations, that it belongs among the books to be kept and cherished.[10]

Rölvaag's ultimate concern in *Giants in the Earth* is not the physical struggle to survive blizzard and plague or the determination to found school, church, and state; instead it is the tension inherent in what Harold Simonson calls the combined "themes of freedom and fate, of society and solitude, of kingdom building and its awesome price."[11] Critics universally recognize that *Giants in the Earth* is unique in presenting the westward movement as a psychological rather than an economic phenomenon. As Vernon L. Parrington points out, most writers before Rölvaag tended to glorify the westward movement as an epic and romantic chapter in American history:

> But the emotional side, the final ledger of human values, we have too little considered—the men and women broken by the frontier, the great army of derelicts who failed and were laid away, like the Norwegian immigrant lad, in forgotten graves. The cost of it all in human happiness—the loneliness, the disappointments, the renunciations, the severing of old ties and quitting of familiar places . . . too often have been left out of the reckoning in our traditional romantic interpretation.[12]

---

10. Carl Sandburg, review in the *Chicago Daily News*, February 11, 1928.

11. Harold P. Simonson, "The Tragic Trilogy of Ole Rölvaag," *The Closed Frontier: Studies in American Literary Tragedy* (New York: Holt, Rinehart and Winston, 1970), p. 78.

12. Vernon L. Parrington, Introduction to *Giants in the Earth* by O. E. Rölvaag (New York: Harper and Brothers Publishers, 1929), p. ix.

## The Cost of the Settlement

Rölvaag expresses the psychological conflict inherent in life on the prairie chiefly through his main characters, Beret and Per Hansa. In them is implicit the dramatic contrast between the "natural pioneer who sees the golden light of promise flooding the wind-swept plain": and the "child of an old folk civilization who hungers for the home ways and in whose heart the terror of loneliness gathers."[13] Beret's frail nature gives way before the overwhelming crudity of life in the wilderness, and she cries out for a godly life, which she believes is attainable only in the old country. Yet her suffering and insanity are not the only tragedy which Rölvaag defines; he is even more interested in the tragic yoking of these two incompatible spirits. Per Hansa's life, activated by a strong sense of mission, demands his participation in the pioneer movement; only on the prairies of the Middle West can his destiny be fulfilled. To yield to Beret's pleadings to return to Norway would mean denying the purpose of his existence, and for Per Hansa such a denial means the soul's death.

Life on the frontier is unendurable for this timid woman whose nature demands the amenities of order, tradition, established law, and custom. Early in chapter 1 we learn that over the arches of the covered wagon are spread two handwoven blankets of such beauty and quality that they "might well have adorned the walls of some manor house in the olden times" (p. 4).[14] Heirlooms, perhaps— certainly among Beret's dearest possessions. She soon finds that on the prairie an unfamiliar set of values exists, and the discovery plunges her into gloom.

The characterization of Beret is a profound study in religious melancholy. Her disorder is not born on the prairie, however. It has its origin far back in her childhood, springing from a dreadful religion of unbridled subjectivism, terror of divine retribution, anxiety, and repression. Of a dark and superstitious nature, she evinces strong signs of morbid pietism early in the book. We learn,

---

13. Ibid.
14. Page references in the text are to the 1927 edition of *Giants in the Earth*.

for example, when Store-Hans in his happiness begins to whistle beside her in the wagon, that she "always objected" to whistling—expressing in her response a fanatical suspicion of merriment, perhaps of music in general.

She dreads the unknown above all things on the prairie—not tangible enemies such as Indians, cold, fire, privation—and lives in terror of the great silence. She shares neither Per Hansa's belief in the healing power of love nor his joy in living because, dominated by fear, she can affirm little except sin and darkness. Rölvaag characterizes the two personalities in a brief exchange:

> "Oh, how quickly it grows dark out here!" the mother murmured.
>
> Per Hansa gave a care-free shrug of his shoulders. "Well," he said dryly, "the sooner the day's over, the sooner the next day comes!" [P. 13]

The difference is unmistakable—Per Hansa confidently accepting his life's mission; Beret terrified of the unknown. In her guilt she wants desperately to hide, imagining that on the open prairie something is about to go wrong.

The first clear sign of her insanity appears while Per Hansa is absent on errands for the settlement. She hangs clothing at the window to shut out the night and shoves the heavy immigrant chest against the door. Her disgust for life on the prairie crystallizes in the view that here men become beasts; first they merely live like animals, burrowing into sod huts, but gradually they disregard moral law and act like animals too. She is convinced that if they remain in the wilderness, everything human in them will be blotted out. Ironically, it is not really the darkness that Beret fears but the light. After Per Hansa whitewashes the interior of their sod hut, she is forced to look downward, finding relief in the shadow of the dirt floor from the brightness of the snow without and the walls within.

Beret conceives of the horizon girdling the prairie as a magic circle, walling them in; nothing good can exist where they dwell.

She imagines that she is in the clutches of the Powers of Evil, that her unhappy life is retribution for giving herself to Per Hansa before marriage and for turning her back upon parents and home to come to America. Yet—and it is this point that lends the sharp edge to the tragedy—her love for Per Hansa demands it all of her, for where he is, "there dwel[ls] high summer." Beret never blames him for her punishment, and her grief is heightened by the knowledge that she is a hindrance to him.

She seeks refuge in the thought of death. She would like to lie with her ancestors, safe at home in the familiar church yard. But she knows that is impossible. Where will they bury her here in the wilderness? They must put her in the old immigrant chest; there she will feel less forsaken and be protected from the wolves. As the months pass, she thinks of nothing except the evil about her—manifest in the weird cloud formations and in the great silence which is life asleep, enchanted.

A comparison of Beret with another victim of religious melancholy—Enok, in Arne Garborg's *Peace*—finds them alike in many respects.[15] After his conversion Enok is up at five o'clock every morning, believing that to lie abed later is to let the flesh conquer. The family begins each day with prayers and hymns, eating their breakfast in silence, for God is always present and must not be offended by idle chatter. The household is silent and unsmiling. "We should never laugh," Enok says; "Jesus never laughed." And he believes it is good to suffer, to be tormented by doubt, for those whom God chastizes, He loves. The one power which might save Enok from insanity is his peasant's love of the soil, but such a love is sinful, for the land is not truly his but God's. After the restoration of her sanity, Beret resembles Enok in her denial of the pleasures of eating and drinking and of natural sexual responsive-

---

15. Arne Garborg (1851–1924) was a Norwegian naturalistic writer, whose work Rölvaag knew and admired. *Peace* (1892) describes his own father's religious struggle, which culminated in madness and suicide. As a teacher of Norwegian literature, Rölvaag undoubtedly was more familiar with masterpieces of Norwegian literature than American.

ness, in her soberness and fanatic insistence upon ritual, and in her disapproval of merriment. And though the conduct of the two households differs in minor points of order, the atmosphere in both is similar. The person responsible for Beret's recovery is the pioneer pastor, who comes to assist in the establishment of a congregation:

> He succeeds in proving to her that the Lord is not the God of wrath, but the kind Father of all living things. She regains reason but becomes a religious fanatic; nothing matters but the preparation for the life hereafter. God has done so much for her, now she must do something for him in return.[16]

The pastor dramatizes his opportunity to help these newcomers bridge the gap between the familiar Old World and the strange American scene by using the immigrant chest as an altar during the first service in the Spring Creek settlement. The chest, introduced early in chapter 1, is a dominant symbol in the book; its inscription, "Anno 16—," emphasizes the continuity essential to the lives of the pioneers. Beret is comforted as she looks upon the consecrated chest, grateful for this affirmation of her belief in the sacredness of her heritage.

By comparison, Per Hansa's religion is an uncomplicated and practical one based on his belief in the goodness of life. He understands the tragedy of his union with Beret but cannot overcome the force which is driving them apart. We sense the gulf between them from the very beginning as he walks ahead of the caravan to avoid answering her questions for which there are no answers. Capable of great tenderness in his relationships with his wife and children, he thinks constantly of pleasing Beret after their arrival at Spring Creek: "Her image dominated all the visions which now seemed to come to him" (p. 46). Nor does Per Hansa escape the longing for home which tortures Beret; his dreams of the future

---

16. Quoted from the copy of press release prepared by Rölvaag describing the meaning of *Giants in the Earth*.

include a great garden on the prairie in which pine trees will be growing—the pines of Norway. The thought always brings tears to his eyes.

After Beret's breakdown Per Hansa confesses to Hans Olsa that what has happened is his fault:

> ". . . I should not have coaxed and persuaded her to come with me out here. [. . .] She is a better soul than any I've ever met. It's only lately that I have begun to realize all she has suffered since we came out here. [. . .] The urge within me drove me on and on, and never would I stop; for I reasoned like this, that where I found happiness others must find it as well."
> [Pp. 416–17]

He has always imposed his will upon life and really understands no other existence. But to Beret there is something sinister in his defiant self-sufficiency. Now here, isolated on the prairie, he even imposes his own law upon men as though he were God. It is this terrible discovery which haunts Beret most persistently and makes her collapse inevitable. Per Hansa's removal of the stakes indicating prior claims to Hans Olsa and Tönseten's land violates a law nearly as old as mankind itself, a law ordained by God: "Cursed be he that removeth his neighbour's land-marks! And all the people shall say, Amen" (p. 155). The fact that the stakes had been placed there before the claimants officially filed their intention to settle absolves Per Hansa legally, but he knows he has committed an immoral act. When the trolls come for restitution, how will it turn out: "Would he be able to hack off their heads and wrest the kingdom from their power?" (p. 125). But he willingly jeopardizes his soul, risking damnation by lying—to save his friends, as he believes, and to prevent a breakup of the settlement. Once the agonizing decision is made, he sleeps "the sleep of the righteous" while Beret lies tormented beside him, wrestling with the knowledge of his guilt.

Not even Per Hansa, to whom "nothing is ever impossible" as far as his fellow settlers are concerned, can survive such an encounter with the trolls: "The Great Plain drinks the blood of Christian men and is satisfied." Before long the two best men in the settlement, Per Hansa and Hans Olsa, are dead; and Beret is left to battle alone the Powers of Darkness.

The origin of Per Hansa can be detected in Chris Larsen in *On Forgotten Paths,* but the prototype is a shell in comparison with the richly conceived Per Hansa. The essential difference between them is that though Chris is suspicious and mean spirited, Per Hansa radiates affection and generosity. Beret and Magdalene are much more strikingly similar. Both are victims of religious melancholy—gentle, fearful, loving beings. And both believe that the prairie calls forth all that is evil in human nature, just as the homeland calls forth all that is good. They imagine their unhappy lives to be retribution for leaving Norway. Like Magdalene, Beret sees visions in which her dead mother speaks to her.

Two motifs woven into the composition of *Giants in the Earth* deserve special comment. The first and most important is the idea of Per Hansa as the *askeladd* of the Norwegian fairy tale. In his optimism he imagines himself in quest of the Castle of Soria Moria; his adversaries on the prairie—storm, misfortune, Beret's illness— are the trolls he must overcome along the way. The novel is full of references to creatures of folklore: gnomes, fairies, and giants. Folklore also provides Beret with her concept of the prairie; she sees the encircling horizon as a magic fairy ring which no living being can enter, like the chain around the king's garden preventing his trees from bearing fruit. She thinks of herself as the only one of the settlers who is really alive; the others are bewitched, lost, dying.

A minor motif—which reappears in *Their Fathers' God*—is the comparison of the Norwegian settlers to the Israelites of old, whom God led into the Promised Land. This idea is given its fullest expression in the sermon of the visiting pastor, who warns that they might either perish, like the ten tribes who turned to idolatry, or inherit the blessings of Canaan as reward for their faithfulness.

Rölvaag loved the novels of the German romanticist Gustav Frenssen (1863–1945), sharing his belief in the essential goodness

## The Cost of the Settlement

of life and in the transforming power of love.[17] *Giants in the Earth* strongly suggests *Jörn Uhl*, Frenssen's most famous novel, in several respects. In *Jörn Uhl* the hero's mother is much like Beret, tormented by the anguish of separation from home and the traditions she loves. Dame Uhl is an alien in the community to which her husband has brought her:

> And she felt in her heart, not for the first time, that she was out of keeping with all this brave show and all this big, noisy house; and her longing soul took flight and flew far away over the marshes and the stunted dry heather, and home to the old farm on the moors. Yes, yes. That was the place for her.[18]

It is Jörn, the son, however, who suffers from religious melancholy. Though he never becomes insane, he comes perilously close to madness—experiences a touch of it—and nearly takes his own life. His restoration comes through the conviction that he must be on the side of God, out of love for God, and seek the good in mankind.

Jörn's love of the old family chest, on which the inscription has become illegible, symbolizes his recognition of ties with the past. But for his father and brothers, the chest has no value, and they relegate it to the stable. Jörn salvages it, cleans and repairs it, and keeps in it his most treasured possessions. The chest stands in his room to remind him of another time, another way of life, another people.

Both novels capture the elemental quality of the satisfied peasant, whose supreme aspiration is to live harmoniously with nature. Jörn is misled by his desire to possess the ancestral farm, The Uhl: it is in reality a desire for power and wealth. He does not achieve serenity until he turns his back upon the rich earth and bountiful

---

17. Colcord was pleased to discover from a letter of Rölvaag's to him that he too had read and loved the novels of Gustav Frenssen. Colcord to Rölvaag, n.d. (written between 1926 and 1928).

18. Gustav Frenssen, *Jörn Uhl*, trans. F. S. Delmer (Boston: Dana Estes and Company, 1905), p. 13.

living of The Uhl to return empty-handed to the ancient home of his mother, its sandy soil offering a bare livelihood but sufficient love to heal all wounds. His life is a quest to discover his mission, and in such a life the seeker must submit to nature:

> "Woe to the man, Jörn Uhl, who is only a hunter after bread, or money, or honor, and hasn't a single pursuit he loves, whereby, even if it be only over a narrow bridge, Mother Nature can come into his life with her gay wreaths and her songs."[19]

This love of the peasant for the earth is as typical of Per Hansa as of Jörn Uhl; both become a part of the land they cultivate. Such a feeling is an Old World characteristic:

> The elemental, the eternal plowman does not belong in American fiction. He is not an American phenomenon. In a country of free land, where nearly every generation of farmers has pulled up stakes and moved on, there can be no question of the European peasant pieties—rooted in endless generations dwelling on the same spot. In Rölvaag the European touch was genuine, because he was dealing with peasants fresh from the European soil.[20]

Critics have tended to think of *Giants in the Earth* as Beret's story primarily, to emphasize the cost of the settlement in terms of human suffering at the expense of the equally important story of man's adjustment to the wilderness. Such a view concludes that the dominant note in the novel is futility:

> Of what avail is the conquest of the soil by man; the scars which man inflicts upon the virgin earth are as nothing to the scars which nature inflicts upon the souls of men.[21]

But Beret, who lives on long after Per Hansa's death, herself becomes a daughter of the prairie, experiencing at times satisfac-

---

19. Ibid., p. 362.

20. "Pioneers," unsigned editorial in *New York Times,* November 7, 1931, p. 18.

21. Henry S. Commager, "Human Cost of the West," *Senior Scholastic* 58 (February 28, 1951): 10–11.

tion—even joy—in accepting the challenge of the frontier. Neither her terrible anguish nor the tragic waste of his life obliterates the import of the final symbol: Per Hansa's body leaning against a haystack, facing west. Surely *Giants in the Earth* records earth's humbling of man, as Commager writes; [22] but just as surely it exalts his incomprehensible courage.

---

22. Ibid., p. 319.

# 6

# THE AFTERMATH:
## peder victorious AND
## their fathers' god

$T$he central character in *Giants in the Earth* is Per Hansa, whose courage, optimism, and joy dominate the action. In the second novel of Rölvaag's trilogy of pioneer life, *Peder Victorious* (1929)—ostensibly the story of Per Hansa's son, the first child born in the Spring Creek settlement—Beret Holm is the major figure, emerging as the fullest, most convincing character Rölvaag ever created.[1] The Beret of this volume is not the brooding fanatic of the earlier book, although melancholy still gnaws at her heart. After her husband's death she finds it necessary to meet life squarely and in the encounter not only holds her own but even exults occasionally in her newly won courage.

In *Peder Victorious* Beret's abundant energy is devoted to rearing her family and managing the large and prosperous farm, but her allegiance to Norway is as strong as ever. Through her Rölvaag reveals an aspect of the process of Americanization different from that which Peder represents. The children of the community are the first to be affected by the new environment, changing more completely and readily than their elders, who have less occasion to change—particularly timid souls like Beret—and who cling to the old with a sense of real need. The strength of Beret's loyalties is suggested by her attention to the ancient cow, Rosie, who was a part of the caravan that pulled into Spring Creek that day back

---

1. O. E. Rölvaag, *Peder Victorious,* trans. O. E. Rölvaag and Nora Solum (New York: Harper and Brothers Publishers, 1929). Published in Norway as *Peder Seier* (Oslo: H. Aschehoug og Co., 1928).

in 1873. Although she long ago passed the age of usefulness, Rosie is treated to a meal of warm gruel morning and evening, in addition to all the corn meal she can eat.

After her husband's death Beret slowly recovers her health and finds a measure of peace. Healing begins when her own sorrow gives way to pity for the helpless widow of Hans Olsa and she brings comfort to that stricken family. During the weeks when she waits for news of Per Hansa, she turns over in her mind again and again her bitter words which drove him into the storm. If it had not been for the pastor's counsel, her mind would have given way under a burden of guilt. Beret finally realizes that her sin is not her cruel behavior that day but rather her chronic discontent. She determines to find the good in life and in her fellow men.

During the summer after Per Hansa's death, she often thinks of Norway and for a time considers returning. But this frail woman, born to follow rather than to lead, whose potentialities remained unfulfilled in the presence of Per Hansa's dynamism, catches a glimpse of the vision which impelled him and finds strength in the thought of the work she must complete on the prairie. Out of the seeming futility of his death comes her restoration to health and her warm response to loyalty and love, as neighbors band together to help with the planting and harvesting that first lonely year.

Almost singly among the immigrants in the Spring Creek settlement, Beret tries to preserve for her family a heritage being lost because of the community's indifference to their Norwegian past. The story of her attempt begins in 1885—four years after Per Hansa's disappearance, when Peder is eleven years old—and covers a period of ten years. Events are considered primarily as they impinge upon the consciousness of Peder, a sensitive and imaginative child, whose personality combines his father's practical concern with life's externals as well as his mother's poetic inclination; yet it is mother and son who are most alike, and Peder must count as his greatest adversary the intense subjectivism characteristic also of Beret.

## The Aftermath

Writing of his materials in the pioneer trilogy, Rölvaag notes:

As I look out over American history I see two chapters stand more boldly against the skyline than all the rest: the Westward Movement and Immigration. These two I tried to reflect in *Giants*. Aside from that I wanted to combine both the plus and minus in terms of the human equation, of this thing that we call Empire-Building. And above everything else I was anxious to make it a *document humaine,* one that should be true for all racial groups, more or less, and endure the acid test of time.

*Peder* deals more with the inner side of the problem. But as I am not half done with him yet, I cannot discuss him objectively. [. . .] Otherwise there is very little that I can say about my books. I have tried honestly to reflect artistically certain passed conditions (or conditions now fast passing) in the history of the Middle West. In both books, and mostly in *Peder,* I set myself the task of building up a soul, using for material the innumerable impressions of the environment in which it grew. I have tried hard to make others understand that which I think I have seen.

*Peder Victorious* is the story of an adolescent boy's development. Commenting on novels which fail to tell the truth, Rölvaag continues:

Take for example the sex urge in normally healthy people: how can it be eliminated from life without committing an unforgivable sin? And why should it be eliminated? But look at how it is being treated—either darkly as something that must be tabooed among decent folks, or it is hinted at lasciviously. The poet of "The Song of Songs" refused to look at it that way; he glorified it, with the result that his poem has been handed down through the ages as one of the finest love songs ever written.[2]

Thus, Peder finds pleasure in his growing sexuality and in the promises of manhood. But *Peder Victorious* is also the story of his

---

2. Rölvaag to Percy Boynton, June 5, 1929. Copy in the Rölvaag Collection.

mixed loyalties and eventual revolt from the life his mother has ordered for him, from the world of tradition and allegiance to his Norwegian heritage to the immediate world of the American language and point of view.

Peder's problems are more acute than those of his brothers and sister, or of most other members of the Norwegian-American community, because his mind is more alert and probing, his responses more sensitive. In his nature converge the tensions of the settlement as it develops from an isolated Norwegian colony on the Middle Western prairie into a thriving American village. The boy is not happy at home, where everything is Norwegian. He senses with shame the differences between his family, especially his mother, and others in the community. In his dreams he lives only in an American world in which he will one day achieve greatness. The mother, still uncomfortable with English after many years in America, insists that Norwegian be spoken in the home and retains as many Old World customs as her children will tolerate. Feeling that they have set themselves apart, Peder longs to embrace absolutely the language and customs of the community. The major problems which Rölvaag explores are Peder's difficulty in reconciling the contradictory demands of home and community and Beret's inability to enter the world toward which he yearns. It is a mistake to assume that in Beret, Rölvaag intends to show the plight of the typical immigrant in the new world. Her mind and heart record an ordeal unknown to less introspective newcomers.

Ever since childhood Peder's questioning mind has refused to be satisfied with passive acceptance of tradition. In parochial school, he aroused the teacher's ire by doubting that Jesus walked upon the water. The old Norwegian schoolmaster contributed to Peder's embarrassment about his heritage, for he was a ridiculous fellow who spoke broken English in an attempt to ingratiate himself with his recalcitrant pupils. Like many an old-timer in the community, he talked about how good life was in the old country. Peder wondered why he did not go back if he liked it so well.

Peder's rejection of the dark religion of his mother, which sees human suffering as the judgment of God upon sinful man, and his adoption of agnosticism is prompted by the community's treatment of an unfortunate neighbor girl. Because she has given birth to an illegitimate child, she is forced to make a public confession before the leering congregation. The episode recalls Rölvaag's youthful indignation when the parishioners at Dönna argued about whether a suicide should be permitted to lie in the hallowed ground of the churchyard. Especially in the character of Pastor Isaksen, Rölvaag criticizes the failure of the church to serve the community effectively. The church is more interested in sermonizing than in ministering, in dogma than in charity.

The incident of the public confessional causes a schism in the Spring Creek congregation; some members believe the penalty is too lenient while others believe it is shamefully harsh.

> Neighbors who formerly had lived peacefully together, and had exchanged work whenever convenient, finding much pleasure therein, would not now look at one another. The threshing seemed so odd that fall: one's nearest neighbor might be working just across the road, and never so much as look up. The ill will abroad changed into hatred; even families were torn asunder. [P. 66][3]

Beret does not side with the separatists, refusing to help tear down what the first pastor had patiently built; but Peder greatly admires the young man who suggests organizing a new congregation and dropping the word "Norwegian" from its name. A new church must be built for the young and for the future, when Norwegian immigrants and their customs will have disappeared from the prairie.

That Rölvaag believed the clergy were not fulfilling their responsibility is clear from several portraits in *Peder Victorious*. The fatherly pastor of *Giants in the Earth*, who brought love and healing

---

3. Page references in the text are to the only English edition of *Peder Victorious*.

to the settlement, meets Rölvaag's standards for the ideal clergyman. Humble, devout, compassionate, he was also the cultural leader of the immigrants. His shortcomings in oratory were trivial compared with his devotion to his people. Beret's religion of fear was abhorrent to him, and he succeeded in opening her heart to the goodness of life.

After his death, this beloved man was replaced by the Reverend Mr. Isaksen, whose qualifications at first impressed nearly everyone except Beret. She thought him a "dolt of a man" in comparison with his predecessor:

> No one had listened to her: people had seemed stricken with blindness. He looked so nice in the pulpit; he had the best of recommendations; he was very well educated; he was so tactful in his associations; he came of good family; and he didn't use tobacco, they had argued. [P. 191]

However, Isaksen's tenure is short: he resigns in despair after provoking the schism which results in the establishment of a rival congregation, and is succeeded by the Reverend Mr. Gabrielson, who is neither so wise as the first pastor nor so hopelessly ineffective as the second. A thoroughly good man, Gabrielson spends his time not in the study but visiting his parishioners to discover their individual needs. But he has a fault which in effect negates the good he does; Gabrielson considers it part of his duty to hasten the dissolution of Norwegian traditions, especially the use of the native tongue, which sets his congregation apart from other Lutheran groups in America. Hence, he preaches in English and discourages the speaking of Norwegian even in the homes, confident—as he is fond of saying—that within twenty years the old language will have been swallowed up by the new.

Nor does the Reverend Mr. Bakken, pastor of the rival congregation, measure up to his duties. His youth, ardor, and fun-loving ways appeal to the young people, and he wins the favor of their elders by defending the Norwegian language. But typical of his superficial approach to the community's problem of acculturation is the series of talks he gives in Norwegian on "Great Men and Notable Events in American History." Peder is too intelligent to be taken in by the politic Mr. Bakken; thus during the critical years when his loyalties might be claimed by the church, he drifts rudderless, encountering no influence outside his home powerful enough to help him withstand the destructive forces inherent in Americanization.

Peder is as irrevocably drawn to the English language and the world it represents as Beret is to the Norwegian. This difference is underlined when he rises in school one evening to recite, in English, the "Gettysburg Address." Uneasily looking over the crowd assembled for a political rally, he seeks out the familiar form of his mother:

> Mother—where was Mother? There, directly in front of him, she sat. He caught her face at a glance, and beheld in it a stranger he had never seen before. Her eyes, wide and kind, had a solemn look, as if she were praying; her sadness [. . .] encircled her face, as the frame of a picture. Now he would show her how beautiful his world really was! [P. 121]

The main speaker of the evening, the flashy and glib Senator McGregor, becomes Peder's idol; the boy vows to speak English someday as beautifully as he does, and never again to utter a word of Norwegian except to his mother. Beret, bewildered and unable to comprehend most of what she hears, feels out of place and views the proceedings with suspicion. After the meeting the teacher, Miss Mahon, detains Beret to tell her how proud she ought to be of Peder and to suggest that she help him overcome his speech difficulty:

> He must by all means get rid of that accent! It would be such a calamity for an American, especially for one with such rare talents, not to be able to speak perfect English! If he didn't get rid of his foreignism now, it might stay with him for life. [P. 138]

Beret understands enough of Miss Mahon's advice to be humiliated and replies angrily in broken English that it is "more important that the boy should learn to understand his own mother than that he should learn to talk nice!" (p. 138).

In the Spring Creek settlement with its immigrant children Miss Mahon is almost militantly devoted to her sacred charge:

> It remained to be seen whether she had sufficient strength to instill in them the very spirit of America—that mighty force which had brought their parents out of bondage in the Old World, had flung wide the doors to this great land, and thereupon had invited the poor and downtrodden to come and be happy in the beauty and promise of the New World. [Pp. 85–86]

She speaks with romantic enthusiasm of the immigrants' gains but is unaware of any cost to them:

> Here they bought, without pay, wine and milk; here they had built, happily confident of the perfect existence to come! All previous history was finished, worn out like an old garment and discarded because no longer usable. [P. 86]

Miss Mahon equates ignorance with ethnic loyalty. Of English ancestry herself, she comprehends nothing of what it means to give up the maternal language. Surely it is only stubbornness which prevents Beret's speaking English fluently and explains her clinging so tenaciously to Norwegian ways.

Unfortunately, the teacher is an ineffective caricature rather than a real person. Like Harry Haugland in *On Forgotten Paths* or Hazel Knapp in *Pure Gold,* she is only a mouthpiece for Rölvaag's impatience with the short-sighted proponents of amalgamation. Chauvinistic, dedicated to perpetuating "the great American tradition," Miss Mahon is enraged to discover a picture, drawn she thinks by Peder, making fun of Washington cutting down the cherry tree:

> At first the shock paralyzed her. Then revulsion set in; righteous indignation seized her, her features hardened! she jumped up, stamped the floor, clenched her hands convulsively . . . . Oh, the contemptible brat . . . the offspring of *that* immigrant

woman! To think that he dared, that he dared to ridicule sacred things in her school! [P. 145] ·

Peder becomes increasingly impatient with his mother's insistence upon their difference from other ethnic groups. His best friend, Charley Doheny, is an Irish-Catholic, and as Peder frequently tells her, "They are *people* too." He does not like to leave the English world of play and school to enter the Norwegian world of home; yet once he has crossed the threshold the change is so natural that he makes it unconsciously:

> "I'll feed the pigs," he said quietly. This was his first utterance in Norwegian since he had left home early this morning; the sound of the words, the sight of his sister and his mother going about doing the work—as they had every day of his life—the sight of the room with all its secrets, obliterated in an instant the whole world in which he had lived so intensely during the day. Here was another world altogether. He had had the same feeling before, but tonight it brought with it such wonder that he had to stop to collect himself. Was it here he belonged, or was it out there in the other world? [P. 106]

The answer to Peder's question, of course, is that he belongs in both of them. Rölvaag implies the folly of the immigrant's cutting himself off from either of these experiences which can enrich his life.

That Peder can so easily reject his heritage to marry his Irish-Catholic sweetheart, Susie Doheny, attests to the failure of church, school, and state to insist upon the special characteristics of immigrant cultures. But in Beret's view the school is the worst offender. Her temporary loss of reason, resulting in her attempt to set fire to the schoolhouse, is not brought on by the discovery that Peder is taking part in a play there, though that fact is shocking enough, but by the discovery of Peder and Susie in each other's arms. The schoolhouse embodies the forces prying him away from her and from the Old World culture, her mainstay in life. Beret's acquiescence in the marriage of Peder and Susie only conceals temporarily the tragedy hidden in their infatuation. In the concluding volume of the trilogy, both of them discover hitherto unrecognized loyalties which prevent a happy union and convince them of the folly of their revolt.

In *Peder Victorious* Rölvaag has written the biography of a settlement rather than a novel. Lacking the elemental drama and poetry of *Giants in the Earth,* the book is likely to be remembered as a survey of changing social conditions in Spring Creek. According to one reviewer,

> [Rölvaag] does not perceive the full value of a scene, of surprise and suspense; and he cannot build with these to produce singleness of effect. On the other hand, the reality, the truth of his work, is beyond question. On relinquishing *Peder Victorious* when the last page has been reached, one has the feeling of having sat at the feet of a very wise and very humane teacher, who has seen and evaluated, and endeavored to express more than he is quite able to express.[4]

*Their Fathers' God* (1931), the third volume of the trilogy, is the story of the unhappy marriage of Peder and Susie, a marriage doomed to failure because of irreconcilable differences in their personality and character.[5] Rölvaag knew that such a story would not have the popular reception of *Giants in the Earth* or even of *Peder Victorious;* moreover, because it dealt with the hostility between Lutherans and Catholics in the Spring Creek settlement, it was certain to arouse controversy. But Rölvaag believed the novel presented a picture essential to understanding immigrant life on the prairie:

> What do I care what the people say about me? I am a lonely soul; I don't belong to any coterie; I am not acquainted with any of the reviewers; the only real friend I have among the writers is Carl Sandburg, and he too lives the life of a hermit. In this book I've sinned gorgeously; I have stepped on a great

---

4. Unsigned review of *Peder Victorious, New York Times,* January 6, 1929.

5. O. E. Rölvaag, *Their Fathers' God,* trans. Trygve M. Ager (New York: Harper and Brothers Publishers, 1931). Published in Norway as *Den Signede Dag* [*The Blessed Day*] (Oslo: H. Aschehoug og Co., 1931).

number of sore corns—I've even bragged of the Jews. [. . .]
But I have the satisfaction of having said things that should
be said according to my way of looking at things; with that
I'll have to be satisfied.[6]

During the months when Rölvaag was working on *Their Fathers'
God,* he was ill and oppressed by the conviction that his life was
drawing to a close. As a result, perhaps, the novel reflects a growing
bitterness and impatience with human folly. He completed the
book uncertain as to whether or not he had accomplished what
he set out to do:

> The mail that took my letter yesterday also took my manu-
> script. Tomorrow it should reach New York. I was glad to
> get the mess out of the house. Last night I think I would have
> sold it for 10 cents. Though the price is just a trifle higher.
> It is very possible that Harpers will turn the manuscript down.
> For one thing, the novel refused to come out in English; and
> for another, the indirect argument against the Catholic church
> may scare them.[7]

Rölvaag was correct in supposing that readers would perceive
that his sympathies were with the Lutheran Beret and Peder rather
than with the Catholic Susie, though his treatment of her spiritual
distress is always compassionate. But it is not primarily his discussion of religious issues that seems inadequate. One reviewer describes the essential weakness of the novel in these words:

> As a story of the differences bred in their believers by two great
> religions, it is sadly superficial, even taking into account that
> the writer wishes to show us these differences only as they
> expressed themselves in the lives of ignorant people. As the
> emotional drama of two loving and unlike personalities, it
> is even more superficial. Irish-Catholic Susie never comes to

6. Rölvaag to G. F. Newburger, October 9, 1931. Copy in the Rölvaag Collec
tion.

7. Rölvaag to G. F. Newburger, June 24, 1931. Copy in the Rölvaag Collection.

life . . . and Norwegian-Lutheran Peder lives chiefly . . . as the son of that lively adventurer, Per Hansa.[8]

The trouble with *Their Fathers' God* is that it is too obviously a problem novel, the characters limited by the ideas they represent. Only Beret escapes the confines of Rölvaag's theories and develops into a free spirit.

After the appearance of *Peder Victorious* in 1928, some readers suggested that Rölvaag had exhausted material of interest in the lives of his Norwegian-American farmers. Rölvaag expresses disapproval of such a view in a letter to Percy Boynton:

> Many reviewers—God bless them! are disgruntled, I notice, with my books because they get so little kick out of reading them. And I presume they are right. There is no great villain in the pictures I have drawn, nor any superhuman hero who can die and get up again as easily as you and I change from our street clothes into our dinner togs and then go to a fine party. Well, I am not interested in that kind of writing. I hate intrigue because it is so vulgarly untrue. How much intrigue is there in the life of decent ordinary country folks? And do our critics mean to say that good folks are not proper subject for literary art? If so, I disagree violently. I tell you, Boynton, there never was a human being that couldn't be made to serve as the best man or the best woman in a novel or a play—given the right interpreter, of course! So divinely interesting is life, so without limit is literary art that every life can be interpreted, and thank God this is true! It certainly is not easy, but it must be possible to tell about an average human being so interestingly that even busy, common folks will stop and listen to the story. The average man is rather plentiful, and that being the case, the writers need not worry about running out of material. Life is beautiful. Why doll it up? And life is certainly dramatic enough as it is—why besmirch it and degrade it?[9]

It was not, however, because Rölvaag used common men and women as subjects that he lost critical favor, but because the special prob-

---

8. Alice Beal Parsons, review of *Their Fathers' God, New York Herald-Tribune,* October 18, 1931.

9. Rölvaag to Percy Boynton, June 3, 1929. Copy in Rölvaag Collection.

lems of adjustment which he considers in his last two novels lack the universal appeal of the westward movement pictured in *Giants in the Earth*. Moreover, characterization has given way to argumentation. The "first faint whine of the problem novel" which Clifton Fadiman detected in *Peder Victorious* is heard even more insistently in *Their Fathers' God*.[10]

The story of *Their Fathers' God* begins in the summer of 1894, a few months after Peder and Susie's marriage, announced at the end of *Peder Victorious*. A terrible drought has stricken the plains, and the town council plans to hire a rainmaker. A handful of men, including Peder, see the folly of such an act and appear at the council meeting to protest. From the beginning Peder is presented as a skeptic, scornful equally of the rainmaker's hocus-pocus and of Father Williams's belief that through such an intermediary, God might choose to perform a miracle.

Peder is scarcely less antagonistic toward the Lutheran clergymen in the district, resenting the timidity which prevents their appearing before the council to challenge the priest and speak out against the rainmaker. It is the duty of the clergy, Peder believes, to assert themselves in the political world; they ought to lead the mob away from its superstitious faith in the rainmaker's promises. Shouted down by the crowd, who want the rainmaker to proceed with his business, Peder adds to his disgrace by getting drunk and staying away from home all night.

Rölvaag wants us to understand the difficulty Peder encounters in translating his idealism into community action. Like Per Hansa, he is concerned mainly with the immediate problems of life. But the novel is also a record of his awakening to the energies of his inner life. Though at first he seems to be primarily a rational being, we discover as his story unfolds that the force which impels him is perhaps essentially imaginative and emotive.

Pride and intolerance are Peder's chief faults. Brutally insensitive to Susie's needs, he respects no kind of mentality except his

---

10. Clifton Fadiman, review of *Peder Victorious*, *Forum* 81 (March, 1929): xx.

own. He is a supreme egoist, believing that the world exists only for those who think and feel as he does. At this stage of his development he is unaware of the possibility of differences in human needs and aspirations. His aim in life, as first expressed in *Peder Victorious,* is to get people to laugh at themselves. And Peder considers mankind's chief folly their dependence upon the past:

> We simply trudge along in the same old ruts, thinking that it's always been this way, and so it's always got to be the same way for ever. Now it's about time we woke up and rubbed the sleep out of our eyes. [P. 32][11]

Like his father, Peder has a sense of his own destiny, which is to goad people into an awareness of their potentialities. But as yet the vision he sees is only of their political and material gains.

Peder is a man of emotional extremes. After drinking himself into insensibility in disgust at the rainmaker's victory over the mob, he vows in shame never to touch liquor again. His relationships with Susie and Beret reveal the same instability, evident also in his lofty but impractical idealism:

> Our task is here to build up a happiness so great and so wonderful that the glory of it will brighten up the far corners of the world. But before we can hope to reach that goal we've got to clear the road of a lot of wormeaten barriers. I mean all those silly superstitions and prejudices that centuries ago should have been dumped into the sea. [P. 55]

Peder is talking, of course, about customs and traditions, which give ethnic groups their cultural distinctness; yet he himself senses that as a Norwegian, he is different from Susie and her people: "She'd never make an Irishman out of me. No Sir, I'm Norwegian, I am!" (p. 59).

His most likeable quality, and one which will see him through the emotional crises that confront him, is his joy in life. In disfavor

---

11. Page references in the text are to the only English edition of *Their Fathers' God.*

with both Susie and Beret after his drunkenness, Peder retreats to
the barn and sinks upon a stool:

> The strong odor of the barnyard, the friendly breathing of
> the cows, and the squirting of the sweet-smelling milk into the
> pail, and the song of a meadow-lark calling its mate today
> affected him strangely . . . . Mother hopping mad . . . . Susie
> crying . . . . Oh well—all the same, life was good . . . an endless
> green meadow where there was naught but kindness. He be-
> longed to the meadow and it to him. Above him lay the blue
> lofts of the heavens . . . one above the other . . . seven in all—
> he had heard Susie say . . . . Seven? . . . It didn't matter. Except
> for the gnawing at the pit of his stomach, life was good and
> kind. A warm sun shed beneficent light down upon every
> creeping thing. [P. 66]

After their marriage, Peder and Susie have moved in with Beret
so that he can help run the farm, the finest one for miles around.
Beret, determined to help them make a success of a bad business,
wins Susie's respect and affection immediately. Peder has always
been scornful of Susie's religious life, which he refers to as
"idolatrous," and his disgust with it deepens when he begins living
with her rosary, crucifix, and ritual. Ignoring his promise to the
priest not to interfere with the practice of her religion, he ridicules
Catholicism at every opportunity.

Peder never quite forgives Susie for siding with Father Williams
over the hiring of the rainmaker, and begins to think of the relationship between the priest and his wife as a conspiracy to overcome
him. Father Williams, believing that one's sole responsibility in
spiritual matters is to acknowledge God and place oneself in the
hands of the church, represents the authoritarianism which Peder
despises. Not certain at all that God exists, Peder insists that man's
business is to ask questions, no matter what beliefs are jeopardized.
He will allow for no intermediary between himself and fortune;
he alone is responsible for his actions.

Peder's hatred of Father Williams and Catholicism increases as
he realizes that Susie's fear of ideas has been bred into her by the

church, and he imagines that it is his duty to tear from her eyes the veil hiding the truth. What Peder does not yet understand is that to destroy her faith would be to destroy her soul. Afraid, like Beret, to launch out into untried realms, Susie needs to live in a familiar pattern.

The basic source of trouble between Peder and Susie, however, is not their religious differences, but the fundamental antagonism between their personalities. Peder is decidedly intellectual in his interests; Susie's orientation is almost entirely physical.[12] Incapable of finding stimulus in Peder's world of thought, she shares with him only a strong sexual need. After their son is born Susie can conceive of no greater joy than to have her child nursing at her breast. During this time when she no longer feels a physical need for him, Peder is excluded from her world and realizes again how tenuous their union is.

After a year with Peder and his mother, Susie still feels like a guest in a strange house. Mother and son converse in Norwegian, which she cannot understand, and she dislikes having to conform to Beret's ways—her methods of cooking, running the household, and doing the chores. Susie never complains that she is treated unkindly by her mother-in-law—indeed, she often refers to her as "the best person in the world"—but Beret's melancholy air, her natural reticence, and her repression of emotion chill Susie's natural gaiety. She resents not being able to display her love for Peder in the presence of his mother, whose nature recoils from any overt expression of sexual interest. For Susie it is perfectly natural to show her emotions, and even Peder is often embarrassed by the openness of her reactions.

Beret's days are happier after the arrival of her grandson. She can take him into her world, though Susie resents it bitterly:

> With her knee swaying to and fro in a cradle-like movement she sang to him strange, sleepy songs, in a language that Susie

---

12. Jorgenson and Solum, *Rölvaag*, p. 416.

could not understand; the words low and soft, the melodies so
sad that all the world's melancholy blinked wide-eyed out of
them . . . . Was this some dark incantation to spirit her child
away and give her a changeling in place? So at least it seemed
to Susie. [Pp. 72–73]

Peder too in the presence of the child slips unconsciously into a
world Susie cannot enter; he has not left behind him the Norwegian
ways of his childhood so completely as he imagines. With his son
in his arms, crooning Norwegian songs, Peder is oblivious to his
wife, who complains of being left out:

"What kind of deviltry are you teaching my chld, anyhow?
Here you were born and raised in this country, same as I was,
and I can't understand a word you're saying. [. . .] How can
he ever learn to talk if you keep this up?" The words were
spoken in a jesting tone, but underneath was a dead seriousness
that was visible in her face. [P. 75]

As the weeks pass, Beret is uneasy because the child has not been
baptized into the Lutheran faith. Susie, growing lax in her religious
duties, does not dare take him to the priest for fear of arousing
Peder's anger. Questioned by his mother about the matter, Peder
is annoyed; to him such a rite is only another superstition. Beret,
brooding about Peder's indifference, determines to have the baby
baptized secretly while Peder and Susie are away. Peder's god-
mother, Sörine, administers the rite, and Beret rejoices to know
that now the child belongs to the Lord.

Learning that her father has been injured and needs help, Susie
goes to him, intending to remain only a few days. On her father's
farm she is happy in familiar surroundings, though the house is
dirty and the buildings are ramshackle. On the way to visit her,
Peder broods about the rift between them, recalling their marriage
day and the promise it held. They were bound for the end of the
world—and Peder is still determined they should reach their goal—
but how much more difficult it really is than he had imagined!
Now his wife is in her father's house, happier than she has been
for a long time:

*143*

Was this Susie? His own wife? By the bed sat a woman whom he recognized but did not know. As for her actions, she might as well have been a stranger. Her father's hand lay in her lap and she was stroking it; in her other arm she had the sleeping boy . . . . What did he have to do with these people? . . . They were only strangers to him . . . of their heart-life he was not a part . . . could never be. [P. 106]

Susie's absence lengthens into months. Her father must be moved into town to be near a doctor's care, and for several weeks they live in the parsonage with Father Williams, where peace abounds:

She felt herself surrounded by an impenetrable wall of goodness. Here she sat among her own people, snug and sheltered in the age-old faith of her fathers. She was theirs and they were hers. Countless, unbreakable bonds held them together. Around them were the great things of life, the things that really mattered, secure and never-failing. A burning desire came to her: If Peder had only been here to experience this hour! And suddenly it was as if she were grovelling about in a strange land where everything was grey and grim. [Pp. 119–20]

The priest tells her kindly but firmly that she is sinning in neglecting her spiritual life because of her husband; he persuades her to have the child baptized without Peder's consent. Like Beret, Susie fears eternal damnation as the vengeance of an angry God. In one way these two women are much alike, both of them timid and superstitious, clinging to a familiar way of life. But Susie is weak, while Beret has strength enough to accomplish the apparently impossible.

Incensed because Susie has been away so long, Peder determines not to ask her to return. Humbled and longing for his embraces, she comes back to the farm one evening, and they are temporarily reconciled. She agrees to remain after finding someone to stay with her father, though she confesses that she does not feel at home here:

Promise that you won't leave me alone at night! I'm afraid of the dark over there. I don't dare sit up in the spooky old loft all alone, with grandma fussing around any hour of the night and making all kinds of weird noises downstairs. She slips in and out the doors so quietly; I get sick with fear and shiver all through. [P. 180]

Living with Susie again, Peder knows their marriage can never be satisfactory. The priest has roused her to an active religious life; she openly performs rituals formerly hidden from view. Because she has no interest in the affairs of the community, Peder cannot share his political activities with her. The discovery that she is pregnant plunges him into even greater gloom but Susie rejoices in her fulfillment. Still, she is not comfortable on Beret's farm. Although Beret is good to her and has given up her room downstairs and moved into the loft, she feels as out-of-place and unnecessary as ever.

Then Peder meets a visiting Norwegian immigrant girl and is immediately attracted to her. Of Lapp ancestry, Nikoline reflects the poetic spirit associated with that nationality. Here, obviously, is a proper mate for Peder. As a newcomer she is dissatisfied with America—people do not know how to have fun—and points to the poverty of its creative life. To her America is characterized by the extremes of vulgarity and religious debauchery. When Peder is with her, he is profoundly aware of their affinities:

> Peder could not understand how any one who sat so still and silent could reach so deep into his heart. Never before had he felt a person's nearness more forcefully. She was sitting here in the dark, she didn't say one word, still she filled his whole being completely. [P. 229]

Through their relationship, based on a sharing of similar interests and ideals, Rölvaag indicates Peder's awakening to the supreme importance of the inner life. He can no longer continue his purely physical relationship with Susie and moves into the loft, leaving her alone in their room downstairs. Nikoline returns to Norway, realizing that it would be disastrous to remain. Although she tells Peder that one should not be afraid to turn back if he discovers he has made a mistake, it seems probable that their relationship ends at this point. Peder has already decided that the memory of her courage gives him strength "to make the journey alone."

After meeting Nikoline, Peder is more receptive to the ideas propounded by the Reverend Mr. Kaldahl, another of Rölvaag's ideal clergymen, who believes in the undiluted transmission of the finest qualities of race. Rölvaag's "racialism" never evolved into a belief in the superiority of the Nordic strain; he asserted only that distinctive characteristics are irrevocably lost in amalgamation. Pastor Kaldahl, a stout defender of everything Norwegian, is an anomaly in a community conditioned to the idea that "foreignisms" are unhealthy in American society.

He tells Peder that it is the responsibility of Norwegian-Americans to cherish and preserve their heritage. "A people that has lost its traditions is doomed!" All American institutions have their roots in the past; among immigrant peoples there can be nothing distinctly American. Norwegians ought to be like the Jews, the pastor continues, preserving their identity and culture in order to make the greatest possible contribution:

> "One thing I see clearly: If this process of levelling down, of making everybody alike by blotting out all racial traits, is allowed to continue, America is doomed to become the most impoverished land spiritually on the face of the earth. [. . .] Gone will be the distinguishing traits given us by God; dead will be the hidden life of the heart which is nourished by tradition, the idioms of language, and our attitude toward life."
> [P. 210]

Peder, thinking of Nikoline and of the Norwegian world he unconsciously enters with his mother and son, finally wonders if it really is possible to be purely American and throw off the influence of the past.

One night Beret falls and breaks her hip. The doctor warns that because her heart has been weakened by a strenuous life, she is not likely to recover. Looking into her ravaged face, he is moved to compassion by the suffering recorded there:

These prairies [. . .] give abundant harvests. Soaked as they are with warm blood, they ought to yield generously. A hell of a price we've had to pay for this empire, and still we can't call it our own. Next time you want someone to rant at your Fourth of July celebration, just call me." [Pp. 243–44]

Beret's last hours are a nightmare to Susie, who is terrified to be with a soul about to enter hell. No priest has come to administer the last rites, and Peder in his anguish seems bent upon flouting God's judgment. Beret, the only one of the characters in the novel who truly lives—too great a soul to be encompassed by the bounds of any argument—in death as in life is a person of dignity and beauty. Confessing her sin in having the child secretly baptized, she asks Susie's forgiveness. But the news shocks Susie so profoundly that she can only taunt Peder with accusations of his mother's wickedness. As bravely as she lived, Beret dies, asking to be buried at the left of Per Hansa, her accustomed place beside him in life.

Hysterical with fear, Susie suffers a miscarriage. Through her long convalescence, Peder is kinder and more loving. But their loyalties conflict again when Peder is persuaded to run for the office of district commissioner. As the campaign progresses, he is dismayed to discover that his Irish opponent's approach is not to argue rationally but to exploit the hostility between Irishman and Norwegian. In a race sparked by bigotry, Peder finally loses the support of his wife, whose choice is determined by nationality and religion. Susie takes the boy and returns to her people, and Peder, having chosen to break with his past, faces the future alone.

If Peder seems to be defeated finally by the hostility of the Irish and the indifference of the Norwegians, sharing a fate "as cruel as the tragedies of Per Hansa and Beret,"[13] one should remember that Rölvaag planned a fourth novel to complete the series about pioneer life. In this book he intended to bring Peder back to the forgotten paths, where he would triumph over the disruptive

---

13. Percy H. Boynton, *America in Contemporary Fiction* (Chicago: University of Chicago Press, 1940), p. 239.

forces of Americanization and fulfill the prophecy inherent in his name: "He was to find himself in terms of his racial heritage and in terms of the new nation he wanted to bring forward and upward."[14]

The Norwegian text of *Their Fathers' God* was ready for the publisher in the spring of 1931; immediately after its completion Rölvaag began work on a translation. The English edition was sent to Harpers on June 23, 1931, appearing on the bookstands October 15 of the same year. During the summer Rölvaag was in exceedingly poor health, suffering one heart attack after another. He longed to enjoy once again the beauty and peace of his north woods retreat, and spent several weeks there with his family during July and August. His letters indicate a renewal of joy:

> [July 30, 1931.] We have spent some very pleasant days up here, listening to the call of the loons, living on fish, after first having had the glorious sensation of pulling them out of the water. There is nothing quite like the summers up in these North regions, they are short and hectic, but have a charm that no other parts in this earth or on it, can have. You ought to see the silver bridge the Green Man up in the sky has during the last few nights been building for us. No engineer could do it as well. And the lapping of the water against the shores of the lake, especially during the last moments of the afterglow when the water turns deep gold, then purple. Such hours there comes over this country a peace "that passeth all understanding." It is *on* this Earth but not *of* it.[15]

> [August 9, 1931.] Thursday night we had a fine rain; there was no wind; the air cleared itself of the heat; until the small hours of the morning I lay listening to the soft, slow, but steady pattering of the rain drops on the roof, and I felt bliss come over me. Finally the clouds broke; the moon came out and silvered the whole earth; and the grey dawn smelt fresh and

---

14. Jorgenson and Solum, *Rölvaag*, p. 427.
15. Rölvaag to G. F. Newburger, July 30, 1931. Copy in the Rölvaag Collection.

fragrant of flowers and of new mown hay. All by myself I had
devotion and felt how good it was to be alive.[16]

On his last day at the cabin, Rölvaag suffered another heart
attack, more serious than any of the previous ones, but he re-
covered sufficiently to attend a meeting of the Norwegian-American
Historical Association in Madison, Wisconsin, in September and
a conference in Chicago the following month. But he knew that
his days would soon be over, and he frequently suffered from pain
and exhaustion. During one such period he wrote:

> It's nothing but a common, ordinary, romantic lie that we
> are the "captains of our own souls"! Nothing but one of those
> damned poetic phrases. Just look back over your own life and
> see how much you have captained! You have been nothing but
> an ordinary hand in the fo'castle. And that's what we all are.[17]

Generally, however, his enthusiasm persisted, and he was determined to work as long as possible. During his last weeks he thought
often of his family in Norway, longing to return for a last visit.
He wrote of this desire to his brother Andreas:

> I have been very poorly. This latest attack brought me
> very close to the shores of eternity, but in the last moment
> the wind turned, and now I lie here butting and chopping
> the breakers. To tell the truth, it is not disheartening to walk
> hand in hand with death. One is bound to be consoled in the
> thought that life makes this unrelenting demand of us all. And
> one does really, in the situation I am in, judge people and life
> in general in a more charitable spirit. All things seem to
> change color; what hitherto meant much comes to be of little
> consequence; nothing seems very urgent.
>
> To be sure I have a great desire to see Rölvaag and the islands
> once more, the people there and especially my own kin, but
> it is not likely that I shall be satisfied in that regard. Even that

---

16. Rölvaag to G. F. Newburger, August 9, 1931. Copy in the Rölvaag Collection.

17. Rölvaag to G. F. Newburger, October 22, 1931. Copy in the Rölvaag Collection.

thought does not cause me great pain. I have never been much afraid of death. Many of my own people have trod the path ahead of me. Hell I have never believed seriously in, at least not in a hell after death. And if there is a better place, I shall meet several there whom I on this earth have loved more dearly than any word can express.[18]

Death came on the afternoon of November 5, 1931, in Rölvaag's fifty-fifth year. Not long before, he had chosen a burial plot on a shady hillside in Oaklawn Cemetery, Northfield, Minnesota, with a view toward the west and the sunset.[19] Here he wished to be laid to rest, identifying himself with Per Hansa, in whose pioneering spirit he found the meaning of life and a promise of better things to come.

---

18. Translated from the Norwegian by Jorgenson and Solum in *Rölvaag*, p. 430.
19. Ibid., p. 431.

# BIBLIOGRAPHY

WRITINGS OF O. E. RÖLVAAG

*I. Published Works*

[Paal Mörck.] *Amerika-Breve*. Minneapolis: Augsburg Publishing House, 1912.

*The Boat of Longing*. Translated by Nora Solum. New York: Harper and Brothers Publishers, 1933. English version of *Længselens Baat*.

*Den Signede Dag*. Oslo: H. Aschehoug og Co., 1931.

*Giants in the Earth*. Introduction by Lincoln Colcord. New York: Harper and Brothers Publisher, 1927. English version of *I de Dage*.

*Giants in the Earth*. Introduction by Vernon L. Parrington. New York: Harper and Brothers Publishers, 1929.

*I de Dage: Fortælling om Norske Nykommere i Amerika*. Christiania: H. Aschehoug og Co., 1924.

*I de Dage: Riket Grundlægges*. Christiania: H. Aschehoug og Co., 1925.

*Længselens Baat*. Minneapolis: Augsburg Publishing House, 1921.

[Paal Mörck.] *Paa Glemte Veie*. Minneapolis: Augsburg Publishing House, 1914.

*Peder Seier*. Oslo: H. Aschehoug og Co., 1928.

*Peder Victorious*. Translated by O. E. Rölvaag and Nora Solum. New York: Harper and Brothers Publishers, 1929.

# Bibliography

*Pure Gold*. Translated by Sivert Erdahl and O. E. Rölvaag. New York: Harper and Brothers Publishers, 1930. English version of *To Tullinger*.

*Their Fathers' God*. Translated by Trygve M. Ager. New York: Harper and Brothers Publishers, 1931. English version of *Den Signede Dag*.

*The Third Life of Per Smevik*. Translated by Ella Valborg Tweet and Solveig Tweet Zempel. Minneapolis: Dillon Press, 1971. English version of *Amerika-Breve*. (The translators are Rölvaag's daughter and grand-daughter.)

*To Tullinger: Et Billede fra Idag*. Minneapolis: Augsburg Publishing House, 1920.

## II. Unpublished Writings

Diary (1896–1901). Translated by Mrs. O. E. Rölvaag.

*Paa Glemte Veie*. English translation by Mrs. C. F. Nickerson.

Rölvaag Collection. Letters, lectures, class notes, diary, newspaper and magazine clippings, manuscripts of the novels, etc., in Archives of Norwegian-American Historical Association, St. Olaf College, Northfield, Minnesota.

*The Romance of a Life*." Rölvaags unfinished autobiography.

## SECONDARY SOURCES

### I. Books

Beyer, Harald. *A History of Norwegian Literature*. Translated and edited by Einar Haugen. New York: New York University Press, 1956.

Björnson, Björnstjerne. *Sunny Hill: A Norwegian Idyll*. Translated from Norwegian. New York: The Macmillan Co., 1932.

Blegen, Theodore C. *Grass Roots History*. Minneapolis: University of Minnesota Press, 1947.

————, ed. *Land of Their Choice: The Immigrants Write Home*. Minneapolis: University of Minnesota Press, 1955.

152

# Bibliography

——. *Norwegian Migration to America: The American Transition.* Northfield, Minn.: Norwegian-American Historical Association, 1940.

——. *Norwegian Migration to America: 1825–1860.* Northfield, Minn.: Norwegian-American Historical Association, 1931.

Boynton, Percy H. *America in Contemporary Fiction.* Chicago: University of Chicago Press, 1940.

——. *The Rediscovery of the Frontier.* Chicago: University of Chicago Press, 1931.

Dasent, George Webbe, ed. *A Collection of Popular Tales from the Norse and North German.* Vol. 13 of *Anglo-Saxon Classics.* Edited by Rasmus B. Anderson. London: The Norrœna Society, 1905.

Frenssen, Gustav. *Jörn Uhl.* Translated by F. S. Delmer. Boston: Dana Estes and Co., 1905.

Garborg, Arne. *Peace.* Translated by Phillips Dean Carleton. New York: W. W. Norton and Company, 1929.

Gvåle, Gudrun Hovde. *O. E. Rölvaag: Nordmann og Amerikanar.* Oslo: University of Oslo Press, 1962.

Ibsen, Henrik. *Brand.* Translated by C. H. Herford. Vol. 3 of *Collected Works of Henrik Ibsen.* Edited by William Archer. New York: Charles Scribner's Sons, 1907.

——. *Love's Comedy.* Translated by C. H. Herford. Vol. 1 of *Collected Works of Henrik Ibsen.* Edited by William Archer. New York: Charles Scribner's Sons, 1907.

Job, Thomas. *Giants in the Earth* [a dramatization]. Introduction by O. E. Rölvaag. New York: Harper and Brothers Publishers, 1929.

Jorgenson, Theodore and Nora Solum. *Ole Edvart Rölvaag: A Biography.* New York: Harper and Brothers Publishers, 1939.

Karolides, Nicholas J. *The Pioneer in the American Novel, 1900–1950.* Norman: University of Oklahoma Press, 1967.

Larsen, Hanna Astrup, ed. *Norway's Best Stories.* New York: W. W. Norton and Company, 1927.

## Bibliography

Lee, Robert Edson. *From West to East: Studies in the Literature of the American West.* Urbana: University of Illinois Press, 1966.

Lie, Jonas. *The Visionary; or Pictures from Nordland.* Translated by Jessie Muir. London: Hodder Brothers, 1894.

Meyer, Roy W. *The Middle Western Farm Novel in the Twentieth Century.* Lincoln: University of Nebraska Press, 1965.

Murray, John J., ed. *The Heritage of the Middle West.* Norman: University of Oklahoma Press, 1958.

Simonson, Harold P. *The Closed Frontier: Studies in American Literary Tragedy.* New York: Holt, Rinehart, and Winston, 1970.

White, George L. *Scandinavian Themes in American Fiction.* Philadelphia: University of Pennsylvania Press, 1937.

*II. Articles and Periodicals*

Baker, Joseph E. "Western Man against Nature: *Giants in the Earth*," *College English* 4 (1942): 19–26.

Beach, Joseph Warren. "Where Men Make Racial Backgrounds Count," *Magasinet,* July 18, 1935.

Beck, Richard. "Rölvaag, Interpreter of Immigrant Life," *North Dakota Quarterly* 24 (Winter, 1956): 26–30.

Boewe, Charles. "An Immigrant Novelist's Views," *Western Humanities Review* 11 (Winter, 1957): 3–12.

Boynton, Percy H. "O. E. Rölvaag and the Conquest of the Pioneer," *The English Journal* 18 (September, 1929): 533–42.

Colcord, Lincoln. "Rölvaag the Fisherman Shook His Hand at Fate," *American Magazine* 105 (March, 1928): 36–37.

Commager, Henry S. "Human Cost of the West," *Senior Scholastic* 58 (February 28, 1951): 10–11.

———. "Literature of the Pioneer West," *Minnesota History* 8 (December, 1927): 319–28.

Fadiman, Clifton. Review of *Peder Victorious, Forum* 81 (March, 1929): xx.

Flanagan, John T. "The Middle Western Farm Novel," *Minnesota History* 23 (March, 1942): 113–25.

# Bibliography

Gray, James. Review of *The Boat of Longing*, *St. Paul Dispatch*, February 1, 1933.

Haugen, Einar. "O. E. Rölvaag: Norwegian-American," *Norwegian-American Studies and Records* 7 (1933): 53–73.

———. "Ole Edvart Rölvaag," in *Dictionary of American Biography* (20 vols., New York: Charles Scribner's Sons, 1928–36), 16: 124–25.

———. Memorial to O. E. Rölvaag, *Nordisk Tidende*, December 3, 1931 (reprinted from *Daily Cardinal* [University of Wisconsin campus newspaper], November 7, 1931).

Heitmann, John. "Ole Edvart Rölvaag," *Norwegian-American Studies and Records* 12 (1941): 144–66.

Hibbard, Addison. "Analysis of *Pure Gold*," *Contemporary Reading: Discussions in Current Literature* 4 (February 15, 1930): 153–69.

Hoidahl, Aagot D. "Norwegian-American Fiction Since 1880," *Norwegian-American Studies and Records* 5 (1930): 61–83.

Interview with O. E. Rölvaag. *Northfield* (Minnesota) *News*, October 8, 1931.

Jorgenson, Theodore. "The Main Factors in Rölvaag's Authorship," *Norwegian-American Studies and Records* 10 (1939): 131–51.

Kaufman, John S. Review of *The Boat of Longing*, *Philadelphia Record*, January 15, 1933.

[Larson, Hanna Astrup.] "Ole Edvart Rölvaag," *American-Scandinavian Review* 20 (January, 1932): 7–9.

Marsh, Fred T. Review of *The Boat of Longing*, *New York Herald-Tribune*, January 22, 1933.

Mirbt, Carl Theodor. "Pietism." *The New Schoff-Herzog Encyclopedia of Religious Knowledge*. Vol. 9. Edited by Samuel Macauley Jackson. New York: Funk and Wagnalls Co., 1908–12.

Olson, Julius E. "Ole Edvart Rölvaag: In Memoriam," *Norwegian-American Studies and Records* 7 (1933): 121–30.

———. "Rölvaag's Novels of Pioneer Life in the Dakotas," *Scandinavian Studies and Notes* 9 (August, 1926): 45–55.

## Bibliography

H. W. P. Review of *The Boat of Longing, Boston Evening Transcript,* January 28, 1933.

Parsons, Alice Beal. Review of *Their Fathers' God, New York Herald-Tribune,* October 18, 1931.

Reigstad, Paul M. "Journey to Rölvaag," *The Norseman,* No. 2 (1967): 56–59.

Sandburg, Carl. Untitled article in *Chicago Daily News,* February 11, 1928.

Sherman, Caroline B. "Farm Life Fiction Reaches Maturity," *Sewanee Review,* 39 (October-December, 1931): 472–83.

Soskin, William. Review of *Pure Gold, New York Evening Post,* February 7, 1930.

Spohn, George W. Review of *The Boat of Longing, Manitou Messenger* [St. Olaf College newspaper], January 17, 1933.

Stegner, Wallace. "History, Myth and the Western Writer," *American West* 4 (May, 1967): 61–62.

Strandvold, George. "Norwegian-American Pride of Ancestry," *American-Scandinavian Review* 34 (September, 1946): 214–19.

*III. Unpublished Material*

Phenneger, Richard Ernest. "The Problems of Self-Realization in the Novels of O. E. Rölvaag." Master's thesis, Washington State College, 1954.

Rölvaag, Mrs. O. E. "Camp Rölvaag." Paper read before Idun Edda, Norwegian society at St. Olaf College, in 1942.

———. Letters to author, February 28, 1956 to May 12, 1958.

Stevens, Robert. "Ole Edvart Rölvaag: A Critical Study of His Norwegian-American Novels." Ph.D. dissertation, University of Illinois, 1955.

Tyler, Frances Lawrence. "O. E. Rölvaag: His Place in American Literature." Master's thesis, University of Missouri, 1950.

*IV. Other Sources*

Rölvaag, Mrs. O. E. Personal interviews during August, 1956, in Northfield, Minnesota.

# INDEX

# Index

# Index

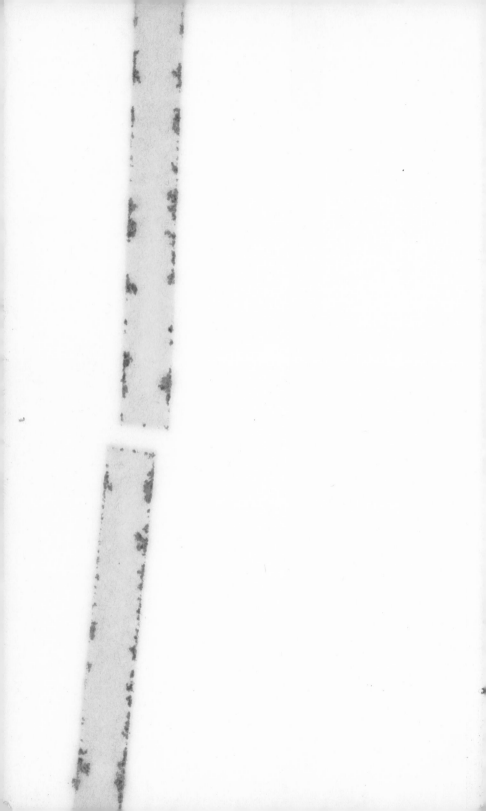